HISTORIES OF THE UNEXPECTED
The Romans

By the same authors

Histories of the Unexpected

In the same series

Histories of the Unexpected: The Tudors
Histories of the Unexpected: The Vikings
Histories of the Unexpected: World War II

HISTORIES OF THE UNEXPECTED
The Romans

Sam Willis & James Daybell

Atlantic Books
London

First published in Great Britain in 2019 by Atlantic Books,
an imprint of Atlantic Books Ltd.
Copyright © Sam Willis and James Daybell, 2019

The moral right of Sam Willis and James Daybell to be identified as
the authors of this work has been asserted by them in accordance
with the Copyright, Designs and Patents Act of 1988.

1 2 3 4 5 6 7 8 9

A CIP catalogue record for this book is available from
the British Library.

Hardback ISBN: 978-1-78649-773-4
E-book ISBN: 978-1-78649-774-1

Printed and bound by CPI Group (UK) Ltd, Croydon, CR0 4YY

Atlantic Books
An Imprint of Atlantic Books Ltd
Ormond House
26–27 Boswell Street
London
WC1N 3JZ

www.atlantic-books.co.uk

For

Kate	*Felix*
&	*&*
Alice	*Bea*

CONTENTS

A Personal Note..................................ix

Acknowledgements...............................xi

The Romans: An Introduction 1

1. Walls 11
2. Tattoos 19
3. Posture 27
4. Taming.................................... 33
5. Recycling 41
6. Walking 49
7. Poison 59
8. The Kiss 67
9. Collecting Art............................. 75
10. Solar Power 83
11. Fish....................................... 91
12. Benches................................... 99
13. Weaving.................................. 107
14. Fattening 115
15. Shopping 123
16. Wicked Stepmothers 131
17. Feet...................................... 139
18. Inkwells 145
19. Demonic Possession....................... 153
20. The Seven Number....................... 161

Selected Further Reading 169

Illustration Credits............................. 187

Index.. 189

Everything

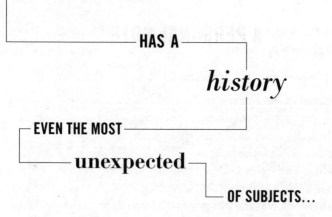

HAS A *history* EVEN THE MOST unexpected OF SUBJECTS...

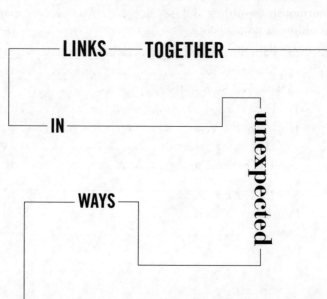

... and *everything* LINKS TOGETHER IN unexpected WAYS

A PERSONAL NOTE

At *Histories of the Unexpected*, we believe that *everything* has a history – even the most unexpected of subjects – and that everything links together in unexpected ways.

We believe that the itch, crawling, clouds, lightning, zombies and zebras and holes and perfume and rubbish and mustard – each has a fascinating history of its own.

In this book we take this approach into the Roman world. You will find out here how the history of *graffiti* is all to do with imperial domination; how the history of *benches* is all to do with public service; and how the history of *inkwells* is all to do with power.

To explore and enjoy subjects in this way will change not only the way that you think about the past, but also the present. It is enormously rewarding and we encourage you all to join in! Find us online at www.historiesoftheunexpected.com and on Twitter @UnexpectedPod – and do please get in touch.

ACKNOWLEDGEMENTS

This series of books is about sharing great research and new approaches to history. Our first acknowledgement, therefore, must go to all of those brilliant historians – professional and amateur – who are writing today and who are changing the way that we think about the past. You are all doing a fabulous job and one which often goes unremarked and unrewarded. Thank you for your time, effort, energy and insight. We could not have written this book without you.

Since this book is intended for a wide and general audience, we have chosen not to publish with extensive footnotes. We acknowledge our indebtedness to fellow historians in the Selected Further Reading section at the end of the book, which is also intended as a spur to further research for our readers.

We would like to thank the many colleagues and friends who have generously offered ideas, guidance, support and sustenance, intellectual and otherwise: Anthony Caleshu, John Daybell (for classical inspiration from a very young age), Bob Higham, Val Maxfield and Derek Gore (for inspiring Sam with the Romans at university), Lee Jane Giles, Beth Robertson, Karen Stears, Jim Holland, Matt Doyne-Ditmas, the Lord John Russell; and among the twitterati, @HunterSJones, @RedLunaPixie, @KittNoir and @Kazza2014.

Collective thanks are also due to Dan Snow, Tom Clifford and the fabulous History Hit team for all their support and encouragement; as well as to Will Atkinson, James Nightingale, Kate Straker, Jamie Forrest, Gemma Wain and everyone at Atlantic Books.

We would also like to thank everyone (and there are hundreds of thousands of you) who has listened to the podcast or come to see one of our live events and been so charming and enthusiastic.

Most of all, however, we would like to thank our families, young and old, for everything they have done and continue to do, to cope with – of *all things* – a historian in their lives.

But we have created this book for you.

Sam and James

Isca – Escanceaster – Exeter
The Feast of St Benedict – 8-Dhū al-Qaʻdah 1440 – I.VII.MMXIX
– 11 July 2019

THE ROMANS:
AN INTRODUCTION

Fresco in the Villa dei Misteri, Pompeii, before 79 CE

WHO WERE THEY?

'The Romans' is a term that is used to describe an enormous number of people who lived in different locations, at different times, under different laws and with different beliefs. As a label, 'Roman' extended well beyond those who were born in or lived in the city of Rome itself. At its height during the second century, under the emperor Trajan (who reigned from 98 to 117 CE), the Roman empire stretched from England in the far north, to modern-day Iraq and the Persian Gulf in the east, to North Africa and Egypt in the south, and Spain in the west. During this period, the empire's population topped 50 million – living within a geographical territory that measured some 2 million square miles, and was around 3,000 miles from east to west. It also encircled the Mediterranean Sea, which the Romans referred to as *mare internum* ('inner sea') or *mare nostrum* (quite literally, 'our sea').

The history of ancient Rome, however, can be divided into several distinct stages. There is the city's birth in the eighth century BCE, related to the founding myth of Romulus and Remus, twin sons of the god Mars; the subsequent 'Time of the Kings' when Rome was ruled by a succession of seven kings from 753 BCE until 509 BCE; and the Roman republic (509–27 BCE), which followed the overthrow of the last king and greatly extended the territory under Roman control. The republic was replaced by an empire in the years 27 BCE–285 CE, during which period it was ruled by emperors. In 285 CE, the empire was split in two, with separate emperors ruling from the capitals of Constantinople in the east and Rome in the west.

From the fourth century, both empires experienced protracted decline lasting for several centuries more. The last recognized emperor of the western Roman empire was overthrown by a Germanic warrior in 476 CE, leaving Rome to a period of barbarian rule which lasted for three centuries, until Charlemagne was crowned king of the Romans in the year 800; but the last recognized emperor of the eastern Roman empire was killed almost a millennium later, when the Ottomans sacked Constantinople in 1453 CE.

The scale of the Roman world – both geographical and chronological – meant that a 'Roman' living in London in 200 CE was very different from a 'Roman' living at the same time in Syracuse or Cologne, or Rome itself, or Alexandria in Egypt; but so too was that 'Roman' living in London in 200 CE different from one living in the same city 153 years earlier, shortly after it was founded in 47 CE, or one living 200 years later when the empire in Britain was still extant, but crumbling. Nonetheless, those who lived under Roman rule at different times and in different locations shared many things, literally and figuratively, as their lives were bound together by Roman government, administration and authority, and were profoundly influenced by Roman technology, culture and trade.

It was an empire based on major cities as well as smaller provincial settlements – built in the Roman style, with local elites governing, issuing laws and edicts, and collecting taxes. The economy was based on trade, taxes and agriculture. Government was based on a unique system of representation, albeit restricted to particular groups – a profoundly new concept for many of the locations that were Romanized.

This all meant that the same Roman living in London in 200 CE, for example, might well know what an amphitheatre, bathhouse and forum were; what a toga was; what *garum* (the Mediterranean fish sauce that flavoured almost all Roman food) tasted like; what a Roman soldier or government official looked like, or even an emperor (from the coins in his or her purse); and might know the value of a good pair of Roman sandals. All of this was knowledge and experience that was shared and replicated for centuries, right across the empire – spread by Roman institutions and classical culture.

CREATING THE EMPIRE

The empire did not simply fall into the lap of Rome, but rather was hard-won through hundreds of years of ferocious fighting and bloody conquest, in which failure was tasted alongside success; the growth of Rome was by no means inevitable. Over several centuries, Rome transformed from a relatively insignificant city to a regional power in central Italy, and by the middle of the third century BCE they had taken over most of the Italian peninsula.

The Punic Wars, a series of three long and protracted wars against the North African city of Carthage, brought significant gains in territory. During these campaigns, the Romans faced fierce opposition – not least in the guise of the commander Hannibal, who during May of 217 BCE attacked the Roman army at Lake Trasimene in Umbria, killing more than 15,000 Roman troops, and in the following year all but destroyed the Roman army, in one battle alone killing more than 50,000 men. After this victory, Hannibal occupied Italy for fifteen years. It was not until the Third Punic War (149–146 BCE) that Carthage was finally defeated, its walls and buildings razed to the ground, its citizens either put to the sword or enslaved. This led to Roman expansion into North Africa and Spain.

During the next century and a half, this expansion in the west was matched in the east as Balkan cities became subject to Rome, and Asia Minor, Syria and Egypt were defeated. In the same period, much of modern-day northern Europe was invaded and conquered to varying degrees.

This impressive territorial empire was built on the back of

the Roman army, which was superbly disciplined, well-equipped and well-led, and which fought with awesome ferocity, clever strategy and utter ruthlessness. The historian Tacitus (56–120 CE) described a Roman campaign in Germania: 'The country was wasted by fire and sword fifty miles round; nor sex nor age found mercy; places sacred and profane had the equal lot of destruction, all razed to the ground.'

This perpetual war machine consumed immense resources, not least humans. During the period of the Roman republic, an estimated half of the male population would have been expected to serve in the army until their mid-twenties – in the later years, before the establishment of the empire, volunteers signed up for sixteen years of service. This system of conscription was replaced by a professional standing army of imperial troops who served for twenty years, with five in the reserves. These extraordinarily high levels of conscription were demanded in order to field the 300,000–500,000 soldiers that guarded the far-flung imperial frontiers through the empire's superb system of paved roads, as well as the sailors that crewed ships patrolling the Mediterranean, Black Sea, English Channel, and Atlantic coasts of Spain and France.

THE EVIDENCE

The vastness of the Roman period has left a bewildering amount of evidence – literary, visual, architectural and archaeological – which has allowed historians to study innumerable aspects of its civilization.

The literary evidence survives in various forms. We have a body of often fragmentary handwritten documents: laws, censuses, tax assessments, lists and even letters, written on papyrus and wooden tablets. One excellent example is a collection of over 750 wooden tablets, some with letters on them, uncovered at the fort of Vindolanda on the northerly frontiers of

Roman Britain, which sheds important light on everyday life in that part of the empire.

Alongside such handwritten documents is an impressive collection of Latin literary texts – histories, essays, poems, plays, manuals and other writings – by giants of Roman literature such as Ovid, Horace, Virgil, Cicero, Martial and Juvenal, almost all of them men. Informative, humorous, cynical and satirical, they offer a vibrant impression of Roman society across the age and of its norms and expectations, as well as anomalies and absurdities of human behaviour.

One of the clearest strands of evidence which both unites these written sources and demonstrates to us a shared Roman culture was their language: Latin. It was the predominant language of the empire, the bureaucratic lingua franca that enforced Roman rule on all provinces, through administration and local law courts. It was expected that all who were freeborn and were enfranchised into the empire should have at least a working knowledge of Latin.

Greek was the other official language, and predominated in the eastern Roman empire and around the Mediterranean as a language of diplomacy. While other languages have left little written record, a wealth of local languages and dialects would have been spoken and written throughout the empire, including Celtic, Punic, Syriac and Egyptian. It was through these languages that an individual living in the empire who did not feel Roman might forge a sense of their own identity.

The physical remains of people as well as objects and arte-facts are also powerful evidence of shared culture, revealing what the Romans wore, ate and used. So too are the magnificent examples of art and architecture that litter the former Roman territories. Paintings, funerary reliefs, sculptures, statues, triumphal arches, civic buildings, temples, villas, roads, walls, aqueducts and fortifications survive as testimony to the reach, technological advancement and cultural sophistication of the Roman civilization.

The combined written and physical record overwhelmingly privileges the lives and experiences of men, who as civic leaders made so much history and had their deeds commemorated in words and stone. It is possible, however, to reconstruct the worlds of a range of Roman women at all social levels, from goddesses and empresses and the wives of politicians, through citizens and freeborn women, to prostitutes and slaves; and in their various social roles as wives, mothers, daughters, kin, lovers, and mistresses of households. Much more challenging to reconstruct are the histories of children, the elderly and the disabled, and the history of sexuality, although a close reading across the sources uncovers fragmentary evidence of a range of groups and experiences.

Taken together, the evidence shows us that ancient Rome was a world of extremes, which makes it seem very human and easy for us to identify with today. Enough survives in the sources for us to see that it was both funny and cruel, violent and peaceful; that people experienced pleasure and pain, want and excess, justice and injustice, rules and judgement; that the Romans were moral and immoral; that it was a period that saw both rapid change and decades of stasis.

STRUCTURE OF SOCIETY

Roman society was rigidly hierarchical. Where you were in the social pecking order affected your everyday life in very tangible ways, from the amount of power and influence you could wield, to who you could marry or the punishments you could receive – as well as what you could wear, eat, and where you could sit in both public and private settings.

The most fundamental legal distinction was between those who were free and those who were slaves. In the Roman world, a slave was either born into slavery or otherwise enslaved through conquest and war. They were the property of their owners, who had the power of life and death over them. Slaves could also be freed, and regularly were.

Those who were free were divided into citizens and non-citizens. Citizens enjoyed legal privileges, including the right to a legal trial and the right to appeal a decision. They could not be tortured or sentenced to death unless found guilty of treason. They could own property and were excluded from certain taxes. They could vote and make contracts. The gift of citizenship was extended throughout the empire as a reward for local families and settlements – sometimes entire cities – and a person could also become a citizen by serving in the army, or be born into it if their parents were citizens. In 212 CE, however, this changed when citizenship was extended to all free inhabitants of the empire by the emperor Caracalla (188–217 CE). Freeborn women were classified as citizens, but although held in high regard they were not allowed to vote or hold public office.

The body of free Roman citizens was broken down further into patricians and plebeians. The former were established land-owning families; the latter the rest of the population who were freeborn. The patricians were subdivided into ranks according to property ownership, with the senators at the top and *equites* below. At the very apex of society were the kings, consuls of the republic, dictators and emperors, who were the political and military leaders of Rome; but from the earliest time of the Roman kings to the thirteenth century in the eastern empire, a varying degree of power lay in the hands of the Senate, the governing body of Rome and a continuous presence and force throughout Roman history.

RELIGION AND BELIEFS

The Roman belief system was polytheistic, which allowed worship of multiple deities, and as the empire's borders grew, so too did the number of religions that were incorporated into it.

This is not to suggest that the Romans simply accepted all religions – as witnessed by their oppression of the Jews and early Christians – but that a range of gods and cults were added to the existing Roman pantheon of gods. Roman mythology included belief in gods such as Jupiter, Juno, Apollo, Mars and Minerva among others, and such paganism was dominant within the senatorial aristocracy and the civil service, as well as in the army.

Perhaps most significant was the impact of Christianity on the Roman empire, which some historians have linked to its decline and eventual fall. In its infancy, Christianity was simply one of a number of religions that offered a mystical union between worshippers and a divine being, with the promise of eternal salvation and the forgiveness of sins.

Despite the early persecution of Christians, their simple message – predicated on personal faith and a relationship with a single god – attracted support first among the poor and slaves, and later within towns and cities. By the second and third centuries CE it had become popular among the civil service and army. A monotheistic religion that was intolerant of belief in competing gods, its success was more or less guaranteed in 312 by the conversion of the emperor Constantine (c.272–337) after his victory at the Battle of the Milvian Bridge, before which he had seen in the sun a cross with the wording 'In this sign, you will conquer'. Constantine's conversion changed the nature of the Roman world forever.

AN UNEXPECTED APPROACH

Traditionally, the history of ancient Rome has been understood in a very straightforward way, following the well-known personalities, events and themes. We think, however, that the period comes alive if you take an *unexpected* approach to its history.

Yes, emperors, armies and the development of civilization all have a fascinating history, but so too do walls, tattoos, collecting art, fattening, recycling, walking, poison, the kiss, posture, solar power, fish, benches, weaving, taming, shopping, wicked stepmothers, feet, inkwells, demonic possession... and even the number seven!

Each of these subjects is fascinating in its own right, and each also sheds new light on the traditional subjects and themes that we think we know so well.

Do you think the Romans are all about conquest, imperial power, and the decline and fall of Rome? Are you ready to build on your knowledge? Then let's start with the history of walls...

·1·
WALLS

Hadrian's Wall at Walltown Crags

Walls are all about Roman subversion...

ROMAN WALLS

Walls were primarily built for protection and privacy – to keep people both in and out. Think here of the massive walls built to surround Rome as a front-line defence during the reign of Aurelian (emperor from 270 to 275 CE) or Hadrian's Wall in the north of Roman Britain, built in the 120s to keep out the Picts.

In buildings, walls were key architectural features for the support of floors or roofs above, but they also delineated space within, and separated the inside world from what was quite literally 'beyond' its walls. Traditionally, then, walls can be viewed as authoritarian structures that sought to order and control, but this was not always the case, and in the Roman world walls and edifices of stone could be used for subversive acts – they were public spaces that could be conscripted for illicit ends.

The physical features of walls themselves – portals, windows, doorways and gates – all offered opportunities for clandestine meetings, while the shadows of high walls allowed people to go unseen. It was in shady corners such as those cast by walls that Seneca (c.4 BCE–65 CE) felt secret acts were to be found: 'pleasure you will most often find lurking around the baths and sweating rooms, and places that fear the police, in search of darkness, soft, effete, reeking of wine and perfume, pallid or else painted and made up with cosmetics like a corpse'.

CLANDESTINE LOVE

It is in the Roman poet Ovid's *Metamorphoses*, however, that the true subversive potential of walls becomes apparent, in his telling

A fresco depicting Pyramus and Thisbe, Pompeii, before 79 CE

of the story of the star-crossed lovers Pyramus and Thisbe. In the story, the tragic pair live in adjacent houses in the city of Babylon. They share a wall but are forbidden to marry by their respective families, who are at war with one another. The story has had many retellings, perhaps most famously in the play-within-a-play in William Shakespeare's *A Midsummer Night's Dream*, but it is with Ovid that the key features of the tale were made available to the Latin-speaking world. The couple are introduced as:

the one the most beauteous of youths, the other preferred before *all* the damsels that the East contained, lived in adjoining houses; where Semiramis [the legendary queen of Babylon] is said to have surrounded her lofty city with walls of brick. The nearness caused their first acquaintance, and their first advances *in love*; with time their affection increased. They would have united themselves, too, by the tie of marriage, but their fathers forbade it. A thing which they could not forbid, they were both inflamed, with minds equally captivated. There is no one acquainted with it; by nods and signs, they hold converse. And the more the fire is smothered, the more, when *so* smothered, does it burn.

Separated by a wall, they are still able to communicate through a chink in its structure:

The party-wall, common to the two houses, was cleft by a small chink, which it had got formerly, when it was built. This defect, remarked by no one for so many ages, you lovers (what does not love perceive?) first found one, and you made it a passage for your voices, and the accents of love used to pass through it in safety, with the gentlest murmur. Oftentimes, after they had taken their stations, Thisbe on one side, *and* Pyramus on the other, and the breath of their mouths had been *mutually* caught by turns, they used to say, 'Envious wall, why dost thou stand in the way of lovers? What great matter were it, for thee to suffer us to be joined with our entire bodies? Or if that is too much, that, at least, thou shouldst open, for the exchange of kisses. Nor are we ungrateful; we confess that we are indebted to thee, that a passage has been given for our words to our loving ears.' Having said this much, in vain, on their respective sides, about night they said, 'Farewell'; and gave those kisses each on their own side, which did not reach the other side.

This wall, then, far from keeping the pair apart, becomes a means of bringing them together, and provides a way in which they can communicate, court each other and fall helplessly in love. Through the chink in the wall they arrange a tryst, which goes terribly wrong, and ends with the pair tragically committing suicide: Pyramus mistakenly thinking his beloved to be dead takes his own life by falling on his sword, while Thisbe enters a short period of mourning only to end her own existence by stabbing herself with the very same sword that mortally wounded Pyramus.

Ovid's *Metamorphoses*

A masterpiece from antiquity. An epic poem consisting of fifteen books completed c.8 CE. The poem consists of around 250 separate myths from the Greek and Roman worlds, each linked by the theme of metamorphosis. It includes stories of men and women changing into various things – including trees, animals and stones – and becoming alien to themselves. Entertaining and charming even to modern audiences, it was written by a man who – seemingly correctly – predicted that his fame would live forever.

THE WRITING'S ON THE WALL

Walls were used in other subversive ways, disconnected from the primary function intended by those who first built them. Throughout history, walls have been surfaces for forms of written or illustrated expression, and the same was true throughout the Roman world, as stone surfaces were scratched, chipped and chiselled with graffiti. Pompeii alone has more than 11,000 examples of graffiti, one of which includes the delightful epigram 'I'm amazed, O wall, that you have not fallen in ruins, you who support the tediousness of so many writers'. This example speaks to the myriad of people who used walls as sites of communication for a whole range of things: eroticism, political dissent, childish play, and messages to family and community.

Different groups – ordinary as well as elite – wrote on walls things with a range of subversive meanings, and it is here that we capture the everyday world of ordinary people living throughout the Roman empire. Graffiti was not simply to be written and then read – there is strong evidence of dialogue between people, usually in the form of an exchange of insults or jests, as in the following inscriptions recorded on the walls of Pompeii. The first reads (loosely translated):

> Successus the weaver is in love with the slave of the
> Innkeeper, whose name is Iris. She doesn't care about
> him at all, but he asks that she take pity on him.
> A rival wrote this. See ya.

What appears to be a riposte to this verse translates as:

> You're so jealous you're bursting. Don't tear down
> someone more handsome—
> a guy who could beat you up and who is darn good-looking.

Yet another riposte is then found on the other side of the door, in which the initial graffiti writer gives his name. It reads:

> I said it. I wrote it. You love Iris,
> who doesn't care about you.
> To Successus, see above.
> Severus.

Clearly this was not the intended purpose of the wall when it was first put up, but through this jocular repartee we are almost able to capture the essence of the Roman conversation – a powerful reminder that walls were used for interactions between everyday citizens, rather than just the elites who wanted to contain them.

PROSTITUTION AND EROTIC WALLS

The subversive markings on walls were often of an erotic or overtly sexualized nature. A Cumbrian quarry first discovered in the eighteenth century and re-excavated in the early 1960s has turned up a range of interesting graffiti, which was made by the team drafted in to make repairs to Hadrian's Wall in around 207 CE. Stone cut from the quarry was used to patch parts of the wall that had fallen into disrepair, and inscriptions by the men who worked there survived, visible to this day. Alongside various inscriptions of officialdom, connected with the third-century campaign to strengthen the border fortifications on the frontiers of the Roman empire, is carved a phallus, which is an erotic symbol of male virility but also a good-luck sign found everywhere across the Roman empire as a way of warding off the evil eye.

One of the most obvious sites for erotic imagery and graffiti, of course, was the brothel. The names and prices of prostitutes were written over the doors of their dwellings, and the remarkable remains of the Lupanar of Pompeii give us a glimpse of the Roman erotic world through the markings and art on its walls. It contains scores of paintings and almost 150 inscriptions, many of an explicit nature – including one that reads simply, and rather proudly, 'I fucked here'. The paintings depict men and women in various sexual positions, one of which features a man encumbered by two large erect phalluses.

It is not uncommon to find the names of male clients and their activities etched into the walls as well: 'Florus', 'Felix went with Fortunata' and 'Posphorus fucked here'; and one particular individual who describes himself as an 'ointment seller', which gives us a more precise idea of the kinds of male clientele who frequented such establishments. Elsewhere, it is possible to reconstruct pricing from the graffiti left behind, with one man etching that he 'had a good fuck... for a denarius'.

THE HOUSE OF MAIUS CASTRICIUS

It is not simply on exterior walls on public streets or in brothels that we find graffiti, however; it also features on the inside walls of domestic dwellings, which were similarly used as sites for self-expression and subversion. An excellent example is the house of the elite Maius Castricius – a Pompeiian site that was excavated in the 1960s. Archaeologists discovered that this four-storey home, which would have overlooked the Bay of Naples, featured some eighty-five graffiti, which were cut into the stucco remains of the walls, around frescoes, in the stairwell, and elsewhere around the home. What emerges from analysis of the various writings and images is the eclectic range of people who seized the building's walls as a site of social engagement and conversation, many of which challenged the formality of the building.

The graffiti depict a riot of interaction that is funny and sociable, while at the same time subversive. Poetic fragments and greetings sit side by side with other graffiti; frescoes alongside rough drawings of a deer, a peacock, a boat, and even the head of a man with what appears to be a phallus extending out of his forehead. Here, too, the romantic and sexual are found, including an elegiac poem that translates as:

> Beautiful girl, you seek the kisses that I stole.
> Receive what I was not alone in taking; love.
> Whoever loves, may she fare well.

In many ways, because the house is an elite dwelling, all the graffiti it contains is subversive – irrespective of what it depicts. It was the action, not the subject, that subverted the social norm.

·2·

TATTOOS

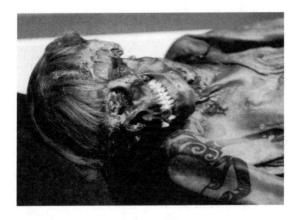

Mummified remains showing a Scythian tattoo

Tattoos are all about imperial dominance...

MARKING SLAVES AND SOLDIERS

One of the ways in which the Romans demonstrated their dominance was their practice of marking different categories of people within the empire, including slaves, soldiers, and people who made military equipment. Tattooing rather than branding appears to have been the most common technique employed, the latter being reserved mainly for indicating the ownership of horses.

Some of the best evidence of tattooing slaves in ancient Rome comes from Petronius's *Satyricon*, which details the antics of the narrator, Encolpius, and his slave Giton.

The two men have both been involved in affairs that turned sour, and find themselves aboard a ship with Lichas – the owner of the vessel, who was infatuated with Encolpius and whose wife Encolpius had slept with – and Tryphaena, a matron and fellow passenger who both Encolpius and Giton had slept with.

Feeling trapped by the situation, there ensues a comic discussion between Encolpius and Giton about how they might escape, either through suicide or through disguising themselves as slaves. In the end they plump for the latter, which involves a manservant shaving their heads and eyebrows. Then the roguish poet Eumolpus suggests a plan involving burnt cork – having discarded the idea of using the ink that he has on board for his writing. He tells the pair:

> [I] will mark your faces with an elaborate inscription to give the impression that you have been punished with a mark. That way the same letters will both allay the suspicions of your pursuers and hide your faces with the appearance of punishment.

Satyricon

A Latin fiction work written in prose and verse by Gaius Petronius (c.27–66 CE) around the middle of the first century. It follows the misdeeds and adventures of the narrator Encolpius and his slave and male lover Giton, as they encounter a series of characters including Eumolpus, a lecherous, aged poet, and Ascyltos, an ex-gladiator and friend of Encolpius. It stands as one of the most entertaining works from the Roman period: a bawdy, irreverent, witty and erotic miscellany.

Encolpius agrees to the plan, describing how 'Eumolpus filled the foreheads of us both with huge letters, and with generous hand covered our whole faces' with a well-known inscription for runaway slaves, which would translate as something like 'Stop me, I'm a runaway'.

The whole plan goes disastrously awry and the escaping pair are caught and brought before Lichas and Tryphaena to answer for themselves, but as the lady views what she thinks are their beautiful faces covered in tattoos, she bursts into tears, demanding to know 'what place of forced labour [they] had fallen into' and who it was who had so cruelly punished them. Lichas, however, is not so easily fooled and bursts out in rage:

> You stupid woman! As if these were wounds prepared with iron so as to absorb letters... they have played a stage-trick on us, and fooled us with mere shadow-writing.

What this comic prose demonstrates is the common practice of tattooing slaves as a mark of ownership, in order to prevent them from running away.

In certain periods of Roman history, former slaves who were freed but nonetheless still bore the markings of their enslaved past enjoyed fewer legal rights than other citizens. As part of legislation passed by the emperor Augustus in 4 BCE, the *Lex Aelia Sentia* restricted the rights of former slaves who had been marked or tattooed on the face. Such people had to remain in an odd limbo status between freemen and slaves, and were not allowed within 100 miles of Rome. If they were caught too close to the city they could be sold, along with all of their possessions.

There is also evidence to show that soldiers and individuals who worked in armaments factories were tattooed. The late-fourth-century Roman writer Vegetius tells of how, after initial military training, recruits were 'inscribed with permanent dots in the flesh' – presumably symbols of the units in which they served. Similarly, a constitution dating from 398 refers to workers in weapons factories receiving a public mark on the arms, similar to that given to recruits, in order that they would not be able to hide if they escaped.

PUNISHMENT

While tattooing was commonly used to mark property, the use of needles and ink on the skin was also employed as a form of penal punishment within Roman society, just as it had been among the Greeks.

In a story told by Valerius Maximus (fl.14–37 CE), a slave belonging to the tribune Antius Restio is punished 'with penalty of chains and with the greatest disgrace to his face, branded with an indelible mark of letters' so he is 'nothing but the shadow and the image of his own penalties'. Philologists debate whether it is branding or actual tattooing that is being referred to here. It is most likely the latter, but in either case it would have been a mark of shame that scarred the face of the slave.

Tattooing was also used to punish and mark criminals. According to the Roman historian Suetonius in his *Lives of the Caesars*, the emperor Caligula 'had many of the better sort first defaced by the marks of tattoos and then condemned them to the mines and the paving of roads'. A legal code from the time of Constantine (272– 337 CE) stated that a person sentenced to become a gladiator should not be tattooed on the face but on the hands or calves, 'so that the face, which has been formed in the image of divine beauty, should be defiled as little as possible'.

Caligula (12–41 CE)

The infamous Roman emperor who ruled from 37 to 41 CE. He was the son of Germanicus, a popular Roman general, and Agrippina the Elder, granddaughter of Augustus, and was a member of the Julio-Claudian dynasty. Although few sources survive from his reign, he gained a reputation for cruelty and extravagance, and was assassinated in 41 CE.

BARBARIANS

While tattooing the face, head, arms, hands and calves was a mark of degradation for slaves, soldiers and weapons workers, there were other peoples in the ancient world – such as Thracians and Scythians – who covered their bodies in decorative tattoos. To the Romans, this was the mark of an inferior civilization, over whom the Romans could assert their dominance.

Designs of fantastical creatures locked in combat or images of birds would have been punctured onto the arms, legs and upper torsos of the Scythians, though given that their bodies were covered in heavy clothing to protect them from the elements (they originated from the area that is now southern Siberia), it is unlikely that they were regularly revealed. A particularly powerful example of this practice survives in a fragment of human skin from a Scythian warrior – now held at the State Hermitage Museum in St Petersburg – that still shows the tattoo of a ferocious tiger.

The ancient Britons were particularly unusual to Roman eyes. When the Romans started to explore Britain from 43 CE onwards, they discovered a people who covered their bodies and faces with blue woad-dye tattoos. Pomponius, the earliest Roman geographer – writing c.43 CE – described the peoples who dyed their bodies as simply 'uncivilized', but a slightly more detailed picture emerges from other sources. Solinus, writing in the early third century, described how they were tattooed from childhood with 'various forms of living creatures... represented by means of cunningly wrought marks' – an idea reinforced in 208 CE by Herodian, who described the tattoos as including patterns and pictures of animals. Herodian believed that this was the reason that the Britons did not wear clothes – 'so as not to cover the pictures on their bodies'.

Caesar, ever keen to see the warlike implications of any cultural practice, noted in his *De Bello Gallico* in the first century BCE how their blue bodies gave them, to his soldiers' Roman eyes, a 'more terrifying appearance' in battle. Certainly the difference between a fully equipped, clothed, shoed and armoured Roman soldier, intent on imperial dominance, and a naked blue warrior could not have been more stark.

TATTOO REMOVAL

Inevitably, considering their association with enslavement, punishment and non-Roman peoples, the removal of tattoos features prominently in Roman sources. The Roman doctor

Aetius described the process of tattooing as 'pricking the places with needles, wiping away the blood, and rubbing in first juice of leek, and then the preparation [a form of ink]', before he offers a vivid description of how to remove them. He outlines two preparations (one lime and sodium carbonate; the other a mixture of pepper, the rue herb and honey) for use in the procedure, prescribing the following:

> when applying, first clean the tattoos with nitre, smear them with resin of terebinth, and bandage for five days. On the sixth prick the tattoos with a pin, sponge away the blood, and then spread a little salt on the pricks; then after an interval... apply the aforesaid prescription and cover it with a linen bandage. Leave on for five days, and on the sixth smear on some of the prescription.

After twenty days, he continues, the tattoos will have disappeared without ulceration or a scar.

Other authors discussed treatments for the removal of tattoos, including the physician and philosopher Galen (who was Greek but lived in the Roman empire) and Pliny the Elder – both of whom recommended using caustic substances. Medical doctors in Rome appear to have routinely operated on people to get rid of tattoos.

Alternative methods involved obscuring the marks – either by bandaging the area or, if on the forehead, growing hair over it in order to cover it. An account by the first-century CE Roman poet Martial of a freed slave trying to pass as freeborn highlights the lengths that people would go to disguise their former situation. He describes how the freeman occupied seats at the theatre normally reserved for senators, dressed in lavish clothes, expensive jewels and scents, and wore a bandage wrapped around his forehead to disguise his lettered slave marks.

·3·

POSTURE

———

Painting from Pompeii, now in the Museo Archeologico Nazionale
in Naples, showing a banquet or family ceremony, before 79 CE

Posture is all about Roman social order...

The human body itself was a form of non-verbal communication throughout the Roman world, and posture – the way people sat, leaned, stood or reclined – was one of the chief ways of distinguishing whether someone was rich or poor, old or young, or of a high or low social standing.

DINING POSTURE

The importance of posture to the social order is beautifully exemplified by the study of Roman dining practices, in particular at the *convivium*. This was the midday or late-afternoon meal, and at its heart was the notion of sociable eating; in the words of the statesman, philosopher and lawyer Cicero (106–43 BCE), the concept of the *convivium* was 'to sit down to dinner with friends because they share one's life'. It was also something of a spectacle, at which to perform and spectate. *Convivium* was a general term for a banquet, the nature of which varied widely. As represented in the dramas of Plautus from the third and second centuries BCE, it was an occasion of companionship in order for men to eat and drink wine together – sometimes in the company of courtesans, with the possible expectation of sex.

At such a meal, there was a discernible hierarchy of postures for men of different social standings, which we see represented abundantly in literary texts, funerary monuments and wall paintings. This is brilliantly demonstrated in a passage from the historian Suetonius's *De Poetis*, which relays an anecdote about the comic Roman playwright Terence, in which, as a young man, he visits the highly respected playwright Caecilius Statius (c.219–c.168 BCE) to read him some of his work.

Suetonius (c.69–after 122 CE)

A Roman author, biographer and historian, primarily known for his work *De Vita Caesarum* (*Lives of the Caesars*) – the biography of Caesar and the subsequent eleven Roman emperors. Suetonius was a friend and protégé of the Roman author Pliny the Younger. He was particularly admired for holding the posts of comptroller of the Roman libraries and keeper of the archives.

The youthful Terence turns up scruffily clad at the senior poet's house while he is dining. Terence is invited to join his host for a meal, but 'because he was poorly clothed' and because of his perceived status as an unknown, he is seated on a bench, near to but separate from his host's couch, upon which the latter is reclining. On reading the first few lines of his verse, Terence so impresses his venerable listener with his elegant words that he is invited to move from his seated position to a couch where he can also recline and share properly in the meal, while continuing to read the rest of his work to his enraptured audience.

Through this we can see how the host reclining on his couch was the centre of the event; that those of similar high status would likewise recline on couches close to the superior male, while those of inferior social status would be placed further from the host, as a mark of their relative insignificance. This particular example is also significant because it shows how important poetry was in Roman society: Terence was allowed to sit close to the host *regardless* of his poor clothing once the value of his poetry was appreciated, and his posture of reclining, once assumed, would have been a far more significant signpost to his status than his attire.

The opposite end of this scale of posture was standing. A relief on a stone altar dating from the second century and now in the Capitoline Museums in Rome depicts an interesting dining experience. In it, the god Orpheus is presented reclining, accompanied by a slave who is standing. The senior male thus reclines, immobile; while the inferior stands, ready to move and do his bidding. This is typical of how slaves were depicted in the Roman world: always on their feet, standing around or else engaged in carrying, serving the guests food and drink or clearing up. An epistle by the satirist Seneca the Younger (c.4 BCE–65 CE) depicts hungry slaves standing silently all evening while their tyrannical master eats and metes out whippings for the slightest noise.

WOMEN AND SITTING

A third figure depicted in the Orpheus relief is a woman. Neither reclining nor standing, she is presented in an intermediate position – sitting – and she is holding Orpheus's hand. She is inferior to the man but superior to the slave, and she is modest in this public setting: the reclining state was linked to female sexual promiscuity. According to Marcus Terentius Varro, writing in the first century BCE and later cited as an authority on outdated dining practices, both men and women originally sat, but afterwards 'men began to recline and women sat, because the reclining posture was deemed shameful in a woman'. This practice of women sitting while men reclined is similarly found in the pages of Valerius Maximus, also writing in the first century CE about 'old Roman customs':

> women ordinarily dined sitting next to men who reclined, a custom that passed from human dining practice to the gods: for at the feast of Jupiter, he himself was treated to dinner on a couch, while Juno and Minerva sat in chairs.

He then explains how this contrasts with the time in which he was writing, a suggestion that women had taken to reclining in their own homes, seen by Valerius as symptomatic of moral decline. It is an important observation that reveals a difference between how women were 'supposed' to behave and how they actually did in practice:

Our own age cultivates this type of discipline more
assiduously on the Capitol than in our own homes,
evidently because it is of greater consequence to the state
to ensure the orderly conduct of goddesses than of women.

Within the literary and visual evidence there are plenty of examples of women who reclined during meals, but these women tended to be prostitutes, actresses, the drunk and the debauched, or women of very high status whose reclining posture often preceded sex.

Varro (116–27 BCE)

A scholar of exceptional learning and repute, but of mixed fortune. Marcus Terentius Varro oversaw the public library in Rome under Caesar but was outlawed under Mark Antony and his books were burned. His works cover an immense array of subjects including jurisprudence, geography, education, astronomy and history, and he wrote in a variety of forms including satires, orations, poems and letters. Only one of his works survives in its entirety: *Res Rustica*, a farming manual.

CHILDREN

Evidence for children's posture is far more limited than that for adults, but from what we have at our disposal it seems that children did not recline. In cases where children were in the company of adults it appears that they sat, and boys only began to recline when they adopted the *toga virilis* ('the toga of manhood') and formally became an adult.

In Suetonius's writings, we learn that the emperor Augustus invited his adoptive sons Gaius and Lucius, along with his own child and the offspring of other aristocratic families, to dinner, making it clear that the young offspring should sit on the ends of their adults' couches. While these children clearly dined at the *convivium*, therefore, it is clear that they were not equal participants in the food and events, by token of their seating arrangement.

A funerary relief dating from the second century CE that survives in Geneva appears to confirm this: a privileged woman is shown reclining, attended by a slave who is standing, as was conventional. But seated nearby is what appears to be a long-haired child. From the woman's body language and the dress of the youth it has been suggested that this does not signify that she is the mother of the child, but conceivably that the figure is some kind of diminutive pet slave with an unusual status as a favourite.

At precisely what age children ceased sitting with adults is uncertain, but Suetonius does offer a clue. A passage concerning the murder of Britannicus intimates that his friend and companion Titus (the future emperor of Rome) was reclining beside him when he drank the poison. We know that Britannicus was near his fourteenth birthday when he died and Titus a year older, which suggests that, as elite males on the verge of adulthood, they were able to practise this adult act.

·4·

TAMING

The Magerius Mosaic, third century CE

Taming is all about courting Roman political favour...

WILD ANIMALS

The Romans were fascinated with the natural world, and that obsession manifested itself in several important ways – one of which was their relationship with exotic or 'wild' animals. The public loved to see such animals. Lions, tigers, leopards, elephants, crocodiles, hippopotami, giraffes, wolves, bears, bulls and rhinoceros were all captured in the deserts, plains and jungles across the empire, and then brought back home and put on display in the city of Rome.

In the capital, providing access to crowd-thrilling, animal-themed spectacles was an important way of courting political favour, raising public support and demonstrating that a politician was attentive to the desires of the masses. For the individual putting on the spectacle, it was also a way of publicly displaying their power, wealth, ingenuity and indeed resourcefulness, for capturing and transporting these animals was a difficult, dangerous and expensive business.

These points are impressively brought together in a mosaic found in North Africa. Dating from the third century CE and discovered in Tunisia, the 'Magerius Mosaic' shows several dramatic scenes of leopards being killed in the arena. In the centre of the mosaic is a steward carrying a tray heavy with bags of coins, and on each side is an inscription commemorating Magerius's munificence and the audience's appreciation of his largesse. It includes the commanding phrase: 'This is what it means to be rich, this is what it means to be powerful, this is the case now.'

Putting on demonstrations of wealth by parading exotic wild animals became so important that they were no mere sideshow

– they were virtually a requirement of anyone with ambitions in public life.

TRAINED TO DIE

As depicted in the Magerius Mosaic, the wild animals could be shown as part of elaborate staged 'hunts' known as *venationes*, in which they were fought and killed for the entertainment of the crowd. They could also be paraded along the streets in processions – or, more rarely, made part of a gruesome spectacle known as *damnatio ad bestias*, in which criminals condemned to death were fed to wild animals as a form of execution.

However one encountered them, these animals were all presented to the Roman public as 'wild' to engender a sense of awe and danger among the onlookers; but all of these beasts had, in some sense, been tamed by Rome. Their very capture and their presence in Rome was a display of imperial strength and tactical and technological ingenuity, as well as geographical reach. As the empire expanded, such animals were brought back as proof of expanding territory and the Roman ability to tame the wild forces – both animal and human – beyond their frontiers.

Once in the city, the animals were often brought even more tightly under Roman control through being trained – a process that sought to produce specific behaviours. Specialists in animal training used simple tricks such as controlling thirst, hunger and temperature, alongside inflicting pain and goading the beasts. The animals could be trained to attack humans; trained to lick humans; trained to attack certain species of animal but not others; they could be trained to pull chariots; trained to do tricks; and trained to do all of this in the heat and noise of an arena packed with humanity.

There was, inevitably, a particular fascination for the occasions when the 'taming' of these beasts failed, and the ordered

Roman world was turned upside down by the ferocity of caged animals. In the *Historia Augusta*, a collection of biographies written down around the fourth century CE, there is an account of lions refusing to fight or even leave their cages, and the slaughter is described as 'providing no great entertainment'; more spectacularly, in Martial's *Liber Spectaculorum*, which recounts the theatrical performances given by the emperor Titus (39–81 CE), a lion turns on its keeper – 'the perfidious lion had injured its trainer in its grim jaws...'

Such failures aside, the man who could provide the most exciting and ingenious entertainment could secure the loyalty of tens of thousands of voters. In a fevered political climate, this inevitably became a competitive business, with rivals trying to outdo each other. The Roman statesman Sulla (c.138–78 BCE) sourced 100 lions for his games in 93 BCE; Pompey had 600 in 55 BCE; and for Caesar's games in 46 BCE some 400 lions were found. It is likely that the beasts were sourced in the locations recently conquered by those generals: Pompey's from Africa and the East; Caesar's from Syria or Mesopotamia; and Sulla's from Mauretania. The demonstration of unusual species was also a part of this popularity contest: Sulla was the first to show a rhinoceros in Rome, and Caesar the first giraffe.

BRUTUS'S GAMES

A significant example of the political importance of wild animal shows comes from the games put on in the spring of 44 BCE by Brutus, one of the leading conspirators in the assassination of Julius Caesar, who was stabbed to death in March of that year. In the aftermath of the murder, the conspirators were forced into exile. Brutus went to Crete but retained his rank as *praetor urbanus*, a title that conferred on him the status of a senior magistrate in Rome, which allowed him to put on games.

Marcus Junius Brutus (85–42 BCE)

A Roman aristocrat and politician, Brutus supported Pompey in his civil war against Caesar but was pardoned. He became governor of Cisalpine Gaul and subsequently an urban *praetor*, just one rank below consul. In 44 CE, Brutus and his fellow conspirators objected to Caesar making himself perpetual dictator and to his deification, and assassinated him in the Theatre of Pompey.

Brutus therefore sought to influence popular opinion by organizing a set of games that took place in his absence but still in his name. At the same time, however, Caesar's adopted heir, Octavian (who became Rome's first emperor, Augustus), planned to put on games to honour Caesar's memory, a ploy to keep his own name in the public eye and to motivate support from Caesar's veteran soldiers.

Thus, the political will of the Roman people was to be pulled this way and that by two sets of games from opposing political camps. As was traditional, Brutus personally oversaw the arrangement of the games, which necessarily included the sourcing of an enormous number of exotic animals trained for the arena. Brutus's games were scheduled first that summer; tellingly, he very specifically ordered his agents to use every single wild animal available in the hunts and in the arena – the clear implication being that none were to be left in Rome for Octavian's games. Cicero later recorded how the public cheered for Brutus at his games; unfortunately, very few sources survive which describe Octavian's games, and none of those mention any animals. The aggressive political manoeuvring seen here in the organization of these games spilled out into civil war, and ultimately led to Brutus's defeat.

WATER AND POLITICS

Another aspect of the taming of the natural world to court political favour can be seen in the Roman management of water. The harnessing of water was one of the most distinctive characteristics of Roman culture, in both city and countryside and in public and private spheres, and can be witnessed across the Roman empire in their hydraulic engineering achievements – in their dams, fish ponds, reservoirs, harbours, aqueducts, bridges, canals, fountains, latrines and bathhouses.

One of the ways in which this is most visible today – and would have been in the past too – is in the network of Roman aqueducts that brought fresh water from distant sources to the towns, cities and harbours. The first aqueduct in the city of Rome, the Aqua Appia, was built in 312 BCE, and by the third century CE the capital alone had eleven. Together they delivered an estimated 1.1 million cubic metres of water per day. Such aqueducts were notable features across the empire, and those that survive are important symbols of Roman civilization. The Valens Aqueduct in Istanbul, for example, still dominates the skyline near Istanbul University; and the multi-arched Pont du Gard in Provence in the South of France, which serviced the Roman city of Nemausus (Nîmes), stretches across the Gardon river and is today one of France's most iconic Roman sites.

Such structures were visible demonstrations of the engineering skills, manpower, finances and raw materials that the empire could wield in order to bend nature to its will. They also permitted a Roman lifestyle – thousands living together in cities, provided with water for drinking, washing and that most Roman of activities, bathing. The wealthy could enjoy fountains and their farmed fish.

More specifically, however, these structures were symbols of a powerful individual: the benefactor or sponsor of that particular scheme. The promise of running water would have been a strong argument for those seeking local election, just as it could be used by emperors seeking to ingratiate themselves with entire regions. Augustus (who ruled 27 BCE–14 CE), for example, was behind the construction of the Aqua Augusta, one of the largest and most complex aqueducts of the time, which supplied water to at least eight entire cities around the Bay of Naples.

Aqua Augusta

Built around 30 BCE to service the many settlements in the Bay of Naples as well as a major Roman naval base at Portus Julius. The main channel was sixty miles long with around fourteen branches, and it filled several substantial reservoirs on the route.

Once in place, the running water itself became a type of political currency. Around 100 CE, a treatise on the Roman aqueduct system was written by the leading engineer and water commissioner for Rome, Sextus Julius Frontinus (c.40–103 CE). Frontinus wrote a two-volume work on the state of Rome's aqueducts at the end of the first century CE, during the rule of either Nerva (ruled 96–98) or Trajan (ruled 98–117). It describes the history of Rome's water supply, as well as technical details such as discharge rates and laws regarding access to water and its use and abuse. We know from this that, in Rome, to draw water from the aqueducts for private use was only achievable with nothing less than permission from the emperor himself.

To have running water in your home in the capital was therefore to demonstrate effectively that you had the emperor's support. In other cities, it could be purchased from the municipal authority – or, if you had achieved something noteworthy, might be granted as a gift; to have running water was in some instances a civic honour. We know, for example, that in 193 CE a wealthy and well-connected man named Titius Chresimus funded a gladiatorial show in the southern Italian town of Suessa Aurunca, and among the civic honours he was granted was a water connection – something which the members of the town council were also granted as a political perk.

The ability to run such systems successfully, however, was so specific to the empire that when the empire collapsed, the aqueducts eventually ran dry, and for several centuries running water in the west was only to be found in monasteries.

·5·
RECYCLING

The Puteoli marble block, preserved at the Penn Museum in
Philadelphia, 95–102 CE

*Recycling is all about Roman
public image...*

The culture of recycling was ubiquitous throughout the Roman empire, as people commonly reused, renovated and repurposed a range of materials – from buildings and arches, to glass and jewellery, to portraits and sculpture. Second-hand markets that sold everything from clothing to antiques were common in the city of Rome, while villas in the countryside were equipped with workshops dedicated to mending and recycling materials.

THE ARCHAEOLOGY OF DISGRACE

Within this widespread culture is the important subject of recycling and repurposing sculptures and architecture that had once been created or raised in honour of a notable individual. Throughout the ancient world, public statuary and architecture were visible symbols celebrating the wealthy benefactors who paid for or commissioned them. Emperors, consuls, senators and wealthy patricians all had statues and civic buildings of varying forms chiselled in their names.

Just as the original creation of such statues or the construction of such buildings projected their benefactors' magnificence, so too did their repurposing or redesigning effectively censure those individuals' memories and identities. This practice, which involved the destruction and confiscation of property, the banning of the use of personal names, and the erasure of names in inscriptions – which was part of what became known to later generations as *damnatio memoriae* (a term not used at the time), a process that saw the removal of the name from all records and official accounts. It was aimed at deliberately obliterating the memory of an individual from the material landscape of the Roman empire.

Domitian (51–96 CE)

Emperor from 81 to 96 CE, Domitian was famed for being loathed by the aristocracy. He was known for cruelty and rapacity, and his severe legislation (including an order to destroy half of all provincial vineyards). Domitian campaigned in person with the army, who loved him – not least for the fact that he raised the army's pay by a full third in 84 CE.

A marble block about five feet high, now preserved at the Penn Museum in Philadelphia but first erected in 95 CE just outside the town of Pozzuoli, near Naples, is an excellent example. It was originally part of a monument dedicated to the emperor Domitian. He fell into disgrace, however, and was assassinated in 96 CE as part of a conspiracy of court officials. After his assassination, the Senate ordered the defacement of all monuments erected to honour his name. A workman armed with a mallet and chisel ascended the monument, and carefully chipped away at each letter of the inscription until it was no longer legible. Interestingly, some letters are completely obliterated while others are partially visible. Archaeologists have suggested that this was the result of the workman's hand getting tired as he hammered away.

Although unreadable to most, modern scholars have managed to decipher the commemorative lines, which read as follows:

To the Imperator Caesar Domitian Augustus Germanicus, son of the deified Vespasian, high priest, in the fifteenth year of his tribunician power, imperator for the twenty-second time, consul for the seventeenth time, perpetual censor, father of the country, the Flavian Augustan Colony of Putoli [dedicates this] having been moved closer to his city by the indulgence of the very great and divine leader.

After his fall from power and the chiselling away of his inscription to erase his memory from history, the same monument was then used for the exact opposite purpose: to honour the new political leadership.

NEW REGIMES

The other side of the marble slab shows how the monument was then repurposed: inscribed into the stone is an image of a Roman soldier and a prefect of the Praetorian Guard (the new emperor's own bodyguard). This was not merely a matter of covering up the identity of a past emperor, therefore, but the clear promotion of a new imperial regime. Rather than wasting perfectly good stone, the monument was recycled to honour and control the public image of the new emperor Trajan, and placed on an arch erected in his honour.

There are many similar surviving examples of sculptures where a face has been cut and altered to take on new features, or a dedication has been changed, or where architectural features have been incorporated into or enhanced as part of new structures, rather than a project being started from scratch.

Paintings too might be modified to incorporate features codifying the power of new ruling elites. Pliny relates the fate of a such a painting, produced by the great artist Apelles (fl. 4th century BCE). His portrait of Alexander the Great captured a personification of war, symbolic of Alexander's celebrated military victories. After many decades on public display, the emperor Claudius (ruled 41–54 CE) commissioned Roman artists to paint over Alexander's face and to set there instead the features of Augustus, the founder of the Julio-Claudian dynasty. In so doing, Claudius was drawing a connection between Alexander's military achievements – and the peace they brought – and Augustus's own *Pax Romana*, or 'Roman Peace'.

Augustus (63 BCE–14 CE)

First emperor of the Roman empire, ruling from 27 BCE until his death in 14 CE, Augustus began his career as a military leader and statesman. It was during his reign that the successes of Rome were consolidated, ushering in a period of relative peace known as the *Pax Romana*, which saw the end of more than 200 years of protracted military conflict. He was the great-nephew of the assassinated Julius Caesar, and helped form the Second Triumvirate to defeat Caesar's assassins.

In a similar way, we can view the repurposing of entire buildings as a means of public-image management, most visible in the changing functions of the great Roman temple, the Pantheon. First funded by Agrippa in around 25 BCE, it is possible that it was originally built as a victory monument after the Battle of Actium (31 BCE). Little is known for certain about its design, but Pliny describes the capitals (decorative tops) of its columns as being 'made of Syracusan bronze', which suggests a certain opulence. This Pantheon burned down in 80 CE and was replaced by a new structure commissioned by Domitian – but this, too, burned down, when it was struck by lightning early in the second century.

The building that survives today dates from the reigns of Trajan and Hadrian in the early second century, when a new building believed to be a temple was constructed on the site of the earlier structures. The present-day Pantheon carries an inscription to Agrippa, the founder of that earlier monument, which reads, 'M·AGRIPPA·L·F·COS·TERTIVM·FECIT' ('M[arcus] Agrippa L[ucii] f[ilius] co[n]s[ul] tertium fecit', which translates as 'Marcus Agrippa, son of Lucius, made [this building] when consul for the third time'). In other words, the structure had been rebuilt by Agrippa when he was consul for the third time.

Subsequent generations of emperors worked to keep the building in good repair, as is attested by brickstamps (which give the date of when they were installed) and other evidence. In 609, it was converted into a Christian church when it was given to Pope Boniface IV by the Byzantine emperor Phocas. Across its lifetime, therefore, the building has been transformed in important ways through restoration and reuse, and had several different functions. It survives today as a church consecrated to 'St Mary and the Martyrs', but to Agrippa it was a victory monument and to Hadrian it may have been a temple, but the preservation of Agrippa's name in the inscription allowed Hadrian to claim affinity with his imperial predecessors.

A PAGAN PAST

Christianity proved another potent force conscious of public image, as Christian Rome sought to disassociate itself from its pagan past while simultaneously appropriating Roman religious sites for Christian uses. All of this happened at a time of anti-pagan legislation which began with Constantine (c.272–337 CE), the first Roman emperor to be converted to Christianity. These laws saw the closing-down of temples, and the confiscation of property and the banning of acts of idolatry. It also led to centuries of temple destruction, including the ancient Greek Serapeum of Alexandria, which in 391 CE was attacked by a mob, sacked and its contents destroyed.

Part of the desire to destroy was a fear of something that was different, an alien culture that was evil and almost *demanded* destruction in order for the new religious regime to be able to assert control. Thus, pagan statues were smashed, burned and broken.

This fear of pagan symbols is clear from an inscription on

the base of a statue in the ancient Greek city of Ephesus, which states:

> Having destroyed a deceitful image of demonic Artemis, Demeas set up this sign of truth, honouring both God the driver-away of idols, and the cross, that victory bringing, immortal symbol of Christ.

Yet Christianity's relationship with the physical remains of Rome's pagan past was not only about destruction, but also taking those spaces over, and repurposing them with a Christian meaning. New churches were built on the exact sites of pagan places of worship, and – just as with the Pantheon – temples and shrines were taken over and consecrated as Christian.

The history of the Santa Maria Antiqua, the fifth-century Christian church built in the middle of the Roman Forum, is another fine example. The church was built on a complex previously commissioned by the first-century emperor Domitian that connected an area near the Temple of Castor and Pollux with the Palatine Hill. Its construction illustrates precisely how the Christian Church sought to redecorate, repurpose and recycle important centres of Roman administration and worship – in this case for the theological and spiritual duties of John VII (c.650–707 CE), the pope who sponsored the project. In so doing, early medieval Roman Christianity – with the papacy at its heart – was symbolically inserted into a space that had once been dominated by its pagan forebears.

·6·

WALKING

Fresco of covered litter carried by workers, Pompeii, before 79 CE

Walking is all about Roman status...

How you walked and with whom you walked said a lot about who you were in Roman society. Walking was a performance, and people constantly assumed that an audience was watching their movements: it was all about seeing and being seen, and was thus fundamental to an individual's identity.

URBAN POWER WALKING

Walking alone was a dangerous occupation in ancient Rome, with its absence of a police force, the massive overcrowding and a constant threat of fire. Under these circumstances, the well-to-do were either accompanied by bodyguards or else by slaves. But more than this, walking with others who were not servants was always a marker of status and power.

Life in the ancient world offered up plenty of occasions where people might be accompanied by a host of followers, whether it be walking in the Forum or around the streets of the capital city, and the size of one's entourage – the number of people who thronged around you as you walked – was a marker of the level of one's social standing and power. In political terms, according to Cicero's brother Quintus Tullius Cicero (102–43 BCE), candidates for office needed to pay heed to the number of their followers, because it was widely taken as a guide of their electoral power. The bigger the entourage, the better you would perform in elections.

Conversely, a small entourage could indicate diminished status or a fall from power, as in the example of the Greek freedman Pallas (d.62 CE), who was secretary during the reigns of Claudius and Nero but was stripped of his office after being implicated in the poisoning of Claudius – along with Agrippina the Younger, with whom he was having an affair. According to the senator and historian Tacitus (c.56–c.120 CE), when Nero had him marched away he mocked him for the size of his entourage, which he suggested was suited to a mere magistrate.

There were a host of ambulatory rituals in Rome that were spectacular processions in themselves, such as at funerals, where entourage again played an important role. One of the chief ways in which power was displayed in this manner was by walking in triumphal entry (a ceremonial entry) into and through the city, as illustrated by the author Pliny the Younger's description of the emperor Trajan's (53–117 CE) first entry into the city:

> Everyone was pleased... that you greeted your clients without prompting and then added some signs of camaraderie. And they were still more pleased that you walked slowly and calmly as far as the crowd of onlookers permitted; that the mob of people thronged around you too, indeed around you especially; that right away, on your very first day, you trusted everyone to be by your side. For you were not surrounded by a band of cronies; instead the finest men of the senate and of the equestrian order spread around you, to the extent that one or the other kind of crowd gained in number, and you followed behind your silent and quiet lictors [bodyguards]. Moreover, the soldiers did not differ from the common people in dress, tranquillity or restraint.

For Trajan, the act of walking through the political capital, Rome, on foot – rather than being carried or riding in a chariot – was an important symbolic act. In so doing, he presented himself as a man of the people, not an aloof emperor, and as someone who was accessible for petitions. Walking through the city thus allowed him to perform a particular role as the most powerful man in Rome.

There were rules and norms for walking, and when they were broken, people could be ridiculed. In one of his epigrams, the poet Martial (c.40–c.104 CE) poked fun at the citizens strutting through Rome, describing one particular man who was peacocking about the streets, walking slowly and ostentatiously, dressed in amethyst, like a sort of ancient Oscar Wilde:

> the *numero uno* of the cloak wearers; the one who is followed by a flock of toga-wearing clients and long-haired slaves and a litter with brand-new linen curtains and leather straps – just a second ago at Caldius's counter he pawned his ring for barely eight cents, so that he could eat dinner.

Here, this man is described for satirical effect – mocked for living beyond his means to appear to his friends as more important than he really was. Clad in the finest clothes and swaggering about with an entourage, he is forced to visit a pawnbroker simply in order to eat.

NOT WALKING

The ultimate statement of power, however, was *not* to walk, but instead to let others – slaves or servants – undertake this menial physical task, and to sit back resplendent and be carried in a litter or sedan, or ride in a chariot through the streets. The use of a litter was not without its detractors, and in some periods the practice was restricted to only the most elite within society. In some circles it even garnered criticism, an example of which comes from a fragment of writing by the politician Gaius Sempronius Gracchus that tells the story of a Roman noble being carried through the countryside. In the tale, a peasant seeing the passing spectacle jokingly asks whether the litter-bearers are in fact carrying a corpse. On overhearing this, the lofty passenger orders his slaves to stop and has the man beaten to death with the very leather straps that tie up the litter.

Gaius Sempronius Gracchus (c.154–121 BCE)

An aristocratic politician of the Roman republic, he was a prominent member of the *Populares* political faction – along with his brother, Tiberius Sempronius Gracchus. His father was consul and his mother was the daughter of the renowned Roman general Scipio Africanus. Elected to the office of tribune in 123 and 122 BCE, his reformist policies created a constitutional crisis, and Gaius committed suicide while being pursued by members of the Senate.

HOW TO WALK LIKE A MAN

The idea that people were defined by their gait is found throughout Roman literature and Roman culture in general, which suggests not only that viewers were able to interpret ambulatory movements, but also that gait was something that could be taught and which obeyed certain rules and consistencies – especially relating to the gender and social status of the walker.

For example, it was prescribed in texts of the period that elite men should walk upright and strong, and be in control of their bodies – for how could a man unable to comport his body properly be able to govern well? Meanwhile, rules about how wealthy men should walk were constructed by a series of negatives – observations on the *opposite* of how they should walk. Specifically, a well-born man should not walk like a slave, a woman or – most importantly – like an effeminate man.

A particular gait was not just a way of demonstrating status but of justifying it. Men of high status were said to have inherited their gait, in much the same way as they might facial features or hair colour: Cleopatra's son Caesarion was thought to have had his father Julius Caesar's gait; while, in mythology, Astyanax was said to have inherited his walk from his father Hector.

Young boys were taught from an early age how to walk, as the satirist Seneca the Younger outlined in an epistle mocking schoolmasters and grandmothers who instructed their pupils in etiquette: 'This is how you walk. This is how you dine. This is proper behaviour for a man. This is proper behaviour for a woman.'

The question of how a Roman man should walk was dependent on precisely who he was. The status of a man was related to how he moved through the city, his house and his gardens. While slaves, for example, were represented as running everywhere in an urgent haste, free citizens moved at a modest pace, and aristocrats, it was felt, should walk slowly with dignity and purpose, and with a controlled and measured gait, since to walk too slow would be to suggest a sluggishness of mind, or the walk of a woman. Cicero, for example, warned his son to:

> be careful neither to employ effeminate lingering in our gait (lest we seem like floats in a parade), nor in our haste to pick up excessive speed; for when that happens our sides heave, our expression changes, our face is twisted: all of which clearly signify that constancy is lacking.

It may be that he felt women walked or were expected to walk slowly, but the key point here is that the aristocratic male walker should neither be excessively slow nor fast, for fear of drawing unwanted attention. The ideal was stately moderation.

The way in which one walked was connected to character by Roman physiognomists, who judged a person's character from their outer appearance. In his work on physiognomy, the second-century rhetorician Polemon wrote: 'Know that length of stride is an indication of loyalty, good counsel, extensive ability, strong-mindedness and anger. They are a people who excel in being with kings.' Effeminate walking was much frowned upon: 'If you see that when he walks he moves his sides and shakes his joints, associate him with fornication, for this is the walk of women.' For Roman men, this sort of gait was seen as overtly homoerotic.

Cicero (106–43 BCE)

A Roman statesman, lawyer, philosopher and orator, Marcus Tullius Cicero was born into a wealthy municipal family of the Roman equestrian order, and is widely considered to be one of the finest Roman orators and prose stylists. He served as consul in 63 BCE and was executed in 43 BCE, having opposed Mark Antony and the Second Triumvirate.

HOW TO WALK LIKE A WOMAN

The way in which women walked was likewise wrapped up in social identity, and observing a woman's gait revealed much about her person.

A sober matron was to be discerned by the moderation with which she deported herself – including the modesty of her gait, which represented a sense of feminine restraint. The opposite end of the spectrum – women walking with wanton extravagance – was to be avoided. According to the poet Catullus (c.84–c.54 BCE), an adulteress was given away by the 'disgraceful' way in which she walked; and Cicero described Clodia Pulchra, daughter of the politician Appius Claudius Pulcher, who was dogged by scandal, as akin to a prostitute in her behaviour:

> if indeed she behaves in such a way – not only in the way she walks, but also in her getup and in her choice of companions; not only by her brazen eyes, not only by her wanton talk, but also by her embraces, by her kisses... she seems to be not just a prostitute, but a rather forward and provocative prostitute...

WALKING WITH FRIENDS

There was a connection in Roman thought, borrowed from the Greeks, between walking and thinking, which was intimately linked to friendship. The culture of walking in ancient Rome was not centred around the strolls of solitude that developed in eighteenth- and nineteenth-century Europe, when leisurely walking took off as a phenomenon. Indeed, the urban promenade (or its rural counterpart, the country ramble) would have held little appeal for the Romans – or, at least, there are few references in the historical record to solitary ambles. Instead, walking in the Roman period was more often a profoundly social activity, connected to friendship – whether it took place in private or in public. As Cicero confided in a letter to his wealthy friend Atticus:

> And so then I wait for you, I miss your company, I even demand your return. For there are many things that are worrying and distressing me, and if I only had your ear, I feel I could pour them all out in one walk's conversation.

This type of walk – the *ambulatio* – was a mixture of mental and physical exercise, though the emphasis was more on the mind than the body. For Pliny, an after-dinner stroll 'with members of

[his] household, among whom there are men of learning' further illustrates the connection between walking, friendship and the intellect, and reminds us that such walks with friends and intimates were very different from the kinds of public walking that took place in the Forum – the public promenades of statesmen surrounded by an entourage of allies, clients and attendants.

·7·

POISON

Wall painting of a woman from the Villa Farnesina, 10 CE

Poison is all about Roman female power...

THE DEADLY ARTS

Poison was commonplace throughout the Roman world, whether used for political ends, to bump off rivals; to rid oneself of unwanted impediments to inheritance, or an unwanted child; or as a method of euthanasia or way of committing suicide. It was used at all levels of society, yet the deadly art of poisoning was a closely guarded secret, a form of dark knowledge that allowed those who owned and mastered it to administer death. Among those most noted for their gifts as poisoners were a number of high-profile women, whose possession of this deadly skill bequeathed to them a peculiarly malevolent form of power.

Several women were well known for their prowess and cunning as professional poisoners. Three of the most infamous, who we know very little about other than their facility as poisoners, were Canidia, Martina and Locusta. The lyric poet Horace (65–8 BCE) presents Canidia as a witch-like old woman possessed of magical powers and suspect morality, who terrorized her victims. She appears throughout his *Epodes* and *Satires* – in one episode, she invades the garden of his patron and rips apart a lamb with her bare teeth, and elsewhere she starves a child to death. She is described as favouring hemlock in honey as a way of dispatching her victims.

In a similar vein, Martina was accused of poisoning the emperor Tiberius's nephew Germanicus, who died in 19 CE in suspicious circumstances. Called to Rome to answer for her alleged crime, Martina died on the journey there – presumably at her own hand, because, as it was reported, traces of poison were found in a knot of her hair.

Agrippina the Younger (15–59 CE)

A woman at the heart of the Julio-Claudian dynasty, Julia Agrippina was the granddaughter of the first emperor, Augustus. She was also the sister of the emperor Caligula and the wife of the emperor Claudius, who was also her uncle. She persuaded Claudius to adopt her son from a previous marriage – Nero – as his heir, thus also becoming mother to an emperor. She was implicated in the death of Claudius, who was poisoned.

Perhaps the most infamous female poisoner, however, was Locusta (d.69 CE), who lived during the first century of the Roman empire. She plied her trade as poisoner-in-chief to various high-ranking Romans, including the empress Agrippina the Younger and her son, the emperor Nero (37–68 CE). She was implicated in attempts to murder Claudius (10–54 CE), Agrippina's uncle and third husband (she was his fourth wife), with a dish of poisoned mushrooms. Nero also employed her services for poisoning Claudius's son Britannicus. The first potion was too weak, but the second was faster-acting and did the trick, greatly pleasing Nero.

As a result of her usefulness to the emperor, Locusta was handsomely rewarded, being provided with vast country estates where she set up a school in order to train others in her techniques. At the school, she and her pupils allegedly experimented on prisoners and animals in order to hone their skills and test out new potions and concoctions.

The methods of poisoning varied widely, from hemlock mixed with honey to poison-tipped needles, which meant that victims died from a simple pricking, none the wiser of who their murderer was. One of the most ingenious techniques was devised by the Egyptian ruler Cleopatra (69–30 BCE), who was renowned for her relationships with Julius Caesar and Mark Antony and has come down to history tainted by her reputation as a cold-hearted tyrant who excelled in poisoning.

Pliny states that Mark Antony was so distrusting of Cleopatra before the Battle of Actium in 31 BCE (which saw rival Roman forces pitted against each other, with Mark Antony's army supported by Egyptian galleys) that he refused all food and drink supplied by Cleopatra for fear of being poisoned. This led to her dipping her ceremonial garland of flowers in poison, and causing the flowers to fall into the wine intended for the Romans. The whole escapade was portrayed vividly by Pliny the Elder:

> Take for example the wicked cleverness of Cleopatra. For in the preparations for the battle at Actium, when Antonius feared even the favour of the queen herself, and did not even take food unless it had been tasted beforehand, she is said to have amused herself with his fear by putting poison on the tips of the flowers in his wreath. Then, as the party went on, she tempted Antonius to drink the wreath. Who would fear such a plot? Therefore she interposed her hand when he went to drink the flowers shredded into his cup and said, 'Well, am I the one, Marcus Antonius, against whom you take the new precaution of taste-testing? If I were able to live without you, would I lack either opportunity or ability?' She ordered a prisoner to drink it, and he died on the spot.

In this episode Cleopatra is not simply represented as an expert in the deadly arts, but also as administering the substance herself, rather than delegating to a servant. This passage perhaps also speaks more broadly to Roman fears of women and foreigners – all of whom were to be distrusted.

POLITICAL CRISIS

The fear of powerful women represented by Cleopatra resonates with other instances of women accused of being poisoners. In many of these cases, the accusations occurred during periods of acute crisis, such as famine or epidemics. Here women – often in positions of influence as the wives of powerful men – were blamed for poisoning large numbers of people. This, of course, was at a time when there was no truly scientific method of proving or disproving whether or not somebody had been poisoned, and so in circumstances of fear and public alarm, women were made the scapegoats – in the same way that they were later accused of witchcraft.

The earliest example of someone being accused of the crime of poisoning occurred in 331 BCE, a year of relatively high mortality which saw the deaths of leading citizens in Rome. These were in all probability due to some form of pestilence, since Rome during this period was overcrowded and disease-ridden. But instead of attributing the cause of these deaths to the unsanitary conditions of the city, the authorities' preferred explanation was poisoning, and after a series of investigations which supposedly stemmed from a tip-off from a slave girl, around twenty women – including wealthy patrician ladies – were accused of brewing poisons. Forced to drink their own concoctions, they all perished at their own hands. While the writer Livy was highly sceptical about the guilt of these women, the hysteria surrounding the deaths in the city and the 'discovery' of these individuals nonetheless led to a further 170 women being found guilty of the same offence and being committed to death by poisoning.

Similarly, in 182 BCE another bout of pestilence wiped out a swathe of important figures in Rome and the surrounding Italian countryside, including magistrates and a consul. So troubling was this, that the Senate ordered an investigation, which resulted in Hostilia, a consul's wife, being charged with committing this crime of mass poisoning of rivals in order to boost the chances of her son rising to the consulship. Again, such charges probably had more to do with male fear of powerful women, and tended to occur during periods of acute crisis, rather than at times of peace and prosperity.

DECADENCE AND DEATH

While it is unlikely that these women were actually mass poisoners, Roman history is certainly full of examples of women who used poison as a weapon to achieve particular political ends, effectively bumping people off in order to further their own interests or those of their families. The Roman satirist Juvenal warned:

> keep watch over your lives; trust not a single dish; those hot cakes are black with poison of a mother's baking. Whatever is offered you by the mother, let someone taste it first; let your trembling tutor take the first taste of every cup.

Juvenal (c.55–c.127 CE)

A Roman poet of the late first and early second century CE, Juvenal was the author of sixteen satirical poems known as the *Satires*, which describe life under the loathed emperor Domitian and focus principally on the corruption of Roman society and mankind's follies. Friend of the poet Martial, Juvenal was a gifted wordsmith, and some of his phrases have survived to the present day in daily language, not least *'Quis custodiet ipsos custodes?'* ('Who will guard the guards themselves?')

In his *Satire VI*, he lists the numerous wives who have done away with their husbands for political reasons. We are told that Caesonia, the wife of Caligula, drove her husband insane by giving him a love potion, and Agrippina murdered her husband Claudius with poisoned food. Juvenal was arguing that poison as a way of achieving personal ends had become something of a status symbol for the elite of Rome.

Another way that Juvenal uses poison to depict a decadent society is in his reference to the use of abortifacients by wealthy Roman women who were either uninterested in caring for offspring or became pregnant by men who were not their husbands:

> So great is the skill, so powerful the drugs, of the abortionist, paid to murder mankind within the womb. Rejoice, poor wretch; give her the stuff to drink whatever it be, with your own hand: for were she willing to get big and trouble her womb with bouncing babes, you might perhaps find yourself the father of an Ethiopian; and some day a coloured heir, whom you would rather not meet by daylight, would fill all the places in your will.

Satire aside, this reference to abortions suggests the power that such poison might have given women in being able to control their own bodies, at a time when influence and politics were located within the family.

·8·
THE KISS

Cupid and Psyche kiss, Museo Archeologico Ostiense,
Ostia Antica, fourth century CE

*The kiss is all about belonging and family
in the Roman world…*

TYPES OF KISSES

Kissing in Rome was a complicated business. In fact, the Romans had three different words for three very different types of kiss: the *suavium*, the lover's kiss; the *basium*, a tender or affectionate kiss on the lips or cheek; and the *osculum*, a kiss of friendship on the lips, forehead or cheek. There were, therefore, different types of kisses to be given in different situations.

There are literary references to kisses between men and women, men and men, women and women; kisses on the eyes, cheeks, lips, feet, hair, head, chest, tongues and genitals; there were kisses that we know as 'blown kisses' – those that shoot through the air, landing with an imaginary smack; and there are even references to lovers kissing inanimate objects if the desired lover was absent – examples include garments, the ground where they once stood, even door posts. There were also secret kisses – the poet Martial wrote in his *Epigrams* (published in Rome between 86 and 103 CE), a fabulous source for understanding the daily life of Romans, about a woman of questionable morality named Fabulla who:

> has found out a way to kiss her lover in the presence of her husband. She has a little fool whom she kisses over and over again, when the lover immediately seizes him while he is still wet with the multitude of kisses, and sends him back forthwith, charged with his own to his smiling mistress. How much greater a fool is the husband than the professed fool!

One of the most important situations in which kisses were exchanged was in greeting. Martial wrote these telling lines about returning to Rome:

> Rome gives you as many kisses as Lesbia did not give Catullus. The entire neighbourhood presses you: the hairy farmer with a goat-smelling kiss; from here the weaver assails you, there the fuller, from here the cobbler having just kissed his hide, there the owner of a dangerous chin... there one with inflamed eyes and a giver of fellatio and recently cunnilingus. Now to return was not worth the price.

Catullus (c.84–c.54 BCE) and Lesbia

The Roman poet Gaius Valerius Catallus referred to his lover in prose as 'Lesbia'. Their relationship was tempestuous, and Catullus's poems are full of disappointment cloaked in sarcasm. Historians believe the identity of Lesbia to be Clodia Metelli, a poet born into a high-ranking Roman family whose life was cloaked in scandal, with numerous accusations of affairs, incest and drunkenness.

Martial also wrote of a man named Titullus who is 'slobbered with kisses of the whole city' and rebukes another, Linus, for forcing people to stop for a kiss of greeting in the winter cold:

> It is winter, and rude December is stiff with ice; yet you dare, Linus, to stop everyone who meets you, on this side and on that, with your freezing kiss, and to kiss, indeed, the whole of Rome. What could you do more severe or more cruel, if you were assaulted and beaten? I would not have

a wife kiss me in such cold as this, or the affectionate lips of an innocent daughter... If, therefore, Linus, you have any sense or decency, defer, I pray you, your winter salutations till the month of April.

Here Martial makes clear that kisses of greeting were impossible to avoid in Rome. Regardless of your professional status – farmer, weaver, fuller or cobbler – and regardless of your health and likelihood of carrying contagion – with your inflamed eyes and 'dangerous chin' – and regardless of what sexual activities you may have been up to, the kiss of greeting identified you as being welcome, as belonging to the Roman 'family'.

A FAMILY CUSTOM

The kiss was also an important activity within each individual family – a means of joining together, of strengthening family bonds across generations and within the sexes. Men would kiss brothers, fathers, sons, uncles and grandfathers just as they would kiss wives, sisters, mothers, daughters, aunts and grandmothers. And to kiss your family members was not just an expectation but – for men at least – a legal right known as the *ius osculi* (the 'right of kissing').

References to the *ius osculi* can only be glimpsed in the sources, but they are telling. The poet Propertius (c.50–c.15 BCE) wrote of falling heavily for a woman named 'Cynthia': 'the first, to my cost, to trap me with her eyes: I was untouched by love before then'. But he soon discovers that Cynthia is less committed than he would have liked: 'Is it true all Rome talks about you, Cynthia, and you live in unveiled wantonness?' Propertius then lets his jealousy overflow, and in doing so gives us a fleeting glance of this legal right to kiss: 'Why, you even invent false relatives, and don't lack for those who have the right to kiss you.'

Suetonius went so far as to suggest that Agrippina the

Younger seduced her uncle, the emperor Claudius (whom she later married), 'aided by the *ius osculi*'. Respectable unmarried women would not have been allowed to be alone with their suitor, but because of this law Agrippina not only could be alone with Claudius but could even show affection towards him in public, a means of disguising their incest. For Roman women, then, the right of kissing could be used to their advantage.

NEW FAMILIES

The kiss was legally – as well as symbolically – significant in the formation of a new family, when a couple were joined together in marriage. Roman marriage was monogamous, with a minimum age for females of twelve and males of fourteen, but betrothal – a promise and legal agreement to marry – could happen from as early as seven years of age. The betrothal was secured with the giving of gifts, ranging from a simple finger ring to livestock, farms and slaves. A kiss, however, was also crucial.

Writing in the third century, the Roman author Tertullian showed that the kiss played a significant role during the betrothal, as well as during the marriage ceremony itself. He claimed that virgins 'have associated with a male by a kiss and [the joining of] their right hands... through the common pledge (*pignus*) of awareness, by which they have fixed the entire union'.

Further details of the legal importance of the kiss in marriage are found in the *Syro-Roman Lawbook*, a fifth-century compilation of legal texts from the eastern Roman empire, which records that a symbolic kiss between a potential bride and her groom was evidence that a betrothal had taken place; indeed, without the kiss, the betrothal was not considered legally binding and annulment could occur without financial implication. Ephrem the Syrian, a fourth-century theologian, supports this idea but makes the kiss even more powerful. In his book *Commentary on Genesis*, Ephrem recounts the Bible story of Jacob and Rachel, a shepherd girl. Jacob arrives in a field where there is a well, blocked by a large stone and surrounded by thirsty sheep. Rachel then arrives with more sheep, 'barefoot and simply dressed, with face burned from the sun, who could not be distinguished from blackened brands that come out of the fire'.

Jacob rolls away the stone, using the power of God inside him. 'And when', continues Ephrem, 'he betrothed [Rachel] to God through [that] marvellous deed, he turned and betrothed her to himself with a kiss.' Here, Ephrem is suggesting that the kiss itself betrothed the woman to her future husband: the kiss was the act that created a family from two individuals.

Tertullian (c.155–after 220 CE)

One of the most important figures in shaping Western Christianity. Born to pagan parents and raised in Carthage, Tertullian travelled to Rome and converted to Christianity on his return, and spent the rest of his life writing. His works are all lyrical and energetic. He wrote in defence of Christianity and tackled theological problems with a conviction and drive that is still discernible in his prose today.

EARLY CHRISTIAN KISSES

The kiss remained highly significant with the rise of Christianity in the Roman empire. In the first five centuries of the new religion, Christians kissed each other in a bewildering number of circumstances, including during prayer, the Eucharist, baptism, ordination, funerals, marriage, the taking of vows and acts of penance. An activity taken directly from the widespread Roman use of the kiss to greet, welcome and form kinship bonds, in this new context kissing helped to bind Christians together into a single unit – into a single 'family'.

This idea of a Christian family was reinforced by rhetoric which spoke of 'brothers and sisters' in Christ. Tertullian made this explicit – explaining that the Christian husband recognized that kissing fellow Christians was analogous to kissing blood relatives: they were all one family. John Chrysostom (c.349–407 CE), Bishop of Constantinople, made the point most eloquently:

> The kiss is given so that it may be the fuel of love, so that we may kindle the disposition, so that we may love each other as brothers [love] brothers, as children [love] parents, as parents [love] children. But also far greater, because those are by nature, these by grace. Thus our souls are bound to each other.

His words were well chosen, as the idea of a familial kiss was so deeply entrenched in Roman society. But here it was now understood that the strength of the bond between Christians was as strong as – if not *stronger than* – that within the family. It is a clever piece of rhetoric, and is testament to how Christianity grew by advertising the value of a profound sense of belonging to a community – symbolized by, and achieved with, a simple kiss.

·9·
COLLECTING ART

Marble statue of a wounded Amazon, 1st–2nd century CE.
Roman copy of a Greek original

Collecting art is all about... Roman identity

ART AND WAR

The Romans were generous in their admiration of art produced by other cultures, and the public display of an eclectic collection of art was a defining feature of the city of Rome. One of the main ways in which it was acquired was as the spoils of war. To seize enemy territory was not enough; to seize its art as well was to literally take possession of its culture, and to capture its soul. Capturing art in this way therefore became symbolic of Roman military might and cultural dominance, both crucial aspects of Roman identity.

Such collecting was particularly noticeable in the aftermath of Roman military victories in Greece in the second and third centuries BCE. Greek cities were then viewed as the centre of cultural sophistication in the Mediterranean – in terms of literature, science and intellectual thought, as well as art. To appropriate Greek art was therefore a powerful and visible demonstration of Rome's military and political domination of this advanced neighbouring civilization.

The origin of the practice is uncertain, but one of the earliest Romans to do so on an enormous scale was the famous general and five-times consul of the republic, Marcus Claudius Marcellus (c.268–208 BCE), who successfully besieged and captured Syracuse in the period 214 to 212 BCE. Syracuse was at that time a Greek city, and its capture led to the first major display of Greek art in Rome. The biographer Plutarch (c.46–120 CE), who was Greek but became a Roman citizen, noted in his biography of Marcellus:

> When Marcellus was recalled by the Romans to the war in their home territories, he carried back with him the greater

part and the most beautiful of the dedicatory offerings in Syracuse, that they might grace his triumph and adorn his city. For before this time Rome neither had nor knew about such elegant and exquisite productions, nor was there any love there for such graceful and subtle art; but filled full of barbaric arms and bloody spoils, and crowned round about with memorials and trophies of triumphs, she was not a gladdening or a reassuring sight, nor one for unwarlike and luxurious spectators.

The actual detail of what was taken does not survive, though the Greek historian Polybius (c.200–c.118 BCE) simply says that he took 'everything'.

The Siege of Syracuse

Fought during the Second Punic War between Rome and Carthage, and particularly notable for the death of the inventor Archimedes, who lived in the city and was killed by a Roman soldier upon its fall. After almost two years of siege, when Syracuse was finally captured, frustrated Roman soldiers looted the city and slaughtered or enslaved its civilians. The fall of Syracuse meant that Sicily became a united Roman province and an important stepping stone to subsequent Roman expansion in Africa and Greece.

The scale of what was plundered in subsequent centuries is astonishing. In 189 BCE, the general and statesman Marcus Fulvius Nobilior (c.231–after 178 BCE) brought back 785 bronze and 230 marble statues, gold crowns totalling 112 pounds, 83,000 pounds of silver, 243 pounds of gold, large quantities of coined money, and arms, armour and artillery from the captured Greek city of Ambracia, once King Pyrrhus's capital. In 146 BCE, the general and consul Lucius Mummius sacked Corinth, which led to one of the greatest hauls of treasure in Rome's entire history. It is recorded that at least 3,000 statues alone were brought back to Rome.

SHARING BOOTY

What happened to such collections of art, gathered together by victorious armies, varied. Lists were made, describing the pieces in detail; even the poses of statues were recorded. If the general responsible for the haul of treasures was granted a 'triumph', he would parade through Rome with his loot vaingloriously displayed for all to see.

Sometimes a part of the spoils was permanently gifted to the people of Rome to decorate the city, creating a unique collection which grew over time with every successive military victory. Art and statues were placed in the Forum, temples, porticoes and other public spaces for the population to see and enjoy. A passage in a compilation of Roman law known as the *Digest of Justinian* even notes that among the possible 'defects' of slaves was being 'addicted to watching the games or studying works of art'.

Modern historians believe that some temples and porticoes would have constituted museums in their own right, containing collections created organically over time – thus not only reflecting Rome's power but also the growth of that power.

After a certain amount had been bequeathed to the city, the remaining captured artwork was ordinarily set aside for the general in charge of the victorious campaign. These pieces were not treated as his personal treasure, but instead were kept as a private collection in his custody – though ultimately intended for public benefit. Such pieces could then be dispersed further afield. Mummius, who captured Corinth in 146 BCE (thus bringing all of Greece under Roman control) was notable for his generosity and for making certain that seized artefacts were not just kept in Rome but were also distributed throughout the empire as a symbol of his powerful reach – travelling as far afield as Spain. Everywhere that a statue went, so too did the message of Rome's triumph and of Mummius's strength; these artworks were messengers of a victorious Roman identity, but also of a specific victorious Roman general's identity.

THEFT, FRAUD AND EXTORTION

It is clear from the writings of Cicero that the expected and appropriate use of the majority of such collections – which, after all, were acquired on behalf of the citizens of Rome – was for the benefit and appreciation of all Romans.

Cicero left us with a detailed account of one of the most unsavoury and unusual characters in the history of Roman collecting, the magistrate and governor of Sicily – and member of the Senate – Gaius Verres (120–43 BCE). Cicero successfully prosecuted Verres in 70 BCE, and subsequently published the speeches he gave in the case as a book, *In Verrem*.

A large – but by no means the only – part of Verres's crimes was the theft of antiques for his own private collection; his several properties were museums in their own right, with exquisite art and statuary featuring throughout the rooms and gardens. Ever-careful with his words, Cicero claimed that Verres had a 'zeal' (*studium*) for collecting, which over time morphed into 'madness' (*amentia*) and 'fury' (*furor*).

Sicily was at this time a crossroads of the Mediterranean, dripping with art, and Verres preyed on both privately and publicly owned artworks, seizing what he wanted and failing to record any of his 'acquisitions'. In his opening speech, Cicero declared:

> I come now to what he himself speaks of as his favourite
> pursuit, his friends as a foolish weakness, Sicily as piracy...
> Even more exactly: in no man's house, even if he had
> been his host; in no public place, even though it was a
> sanctuary; in the possession of no one, whether Sicilian or
> Roman citizen; whether public or private property, whether
> consecrated or not consecrated, nowhere in all of Sicily has
> he left anything that he saw and wanted.

Among the treasures Verres stole for himself was a statue of Jupiter Imperator from its temple, which Cicero claimed was among the three most magnificent statues of Jupiter in the world. Other notable acquisitions were statues of Paean and Aristaeus from the temples of Liber and Bacchus, and a series of paintings from Minerva's temple that depicted a cavalry engagement of Agathocles, King of Syracuse (317–289 BCE).

Verres's collecting was certainly unusual in its scope, and his reputation for such criminal activity is what brought him to Cicero's attention in the first place. Cicero was then a little-known lawyer with big aspirations, and he fell on Verres with the full force of his intellect and rhetoric as a way of securing public support for his own political career. Here was a man who, under the Roman system of administration and governance, was empowered to guarantee the island's stability and security, and yet he had undermined it by using that very power to plunder communities and strip temples for his own benefit.

In Cicero's eyes, Verres's behaviour challenged ideals of how Roman officials should behave, and the relationship with art was an important part of this. Accumulating art was viewed as an admirable activity; indeed, Cicero was a collector himself. But he was of the opinion that this should be done in an appropriate way that reflected positively on one's identity as a Roman. While acquisitions gained through war – if properly catalogued and archived – were fine, using public office to despoil communities was not. Moreover, the purpose of collecting was connoisseurship, not to acquire wealth, satisfy greed or covet the property of another; and art acquired from a position of public power needed to be shared in public buildings.

In reality, not all Romans who acquired art when in positions of power acted in as civic-minded a manner, but Cicero's vision of ideal behaviour as set out in his opening speech, along with the evidence he provided, was so damning that Verres immediately went into voluntary exile.

·10·
SOLAR POWER

Inside the Pantheon in Rome, the church of St Mary and the Martyrs
since the seventh century CE

*Solar power is all about Roman
architecture…*

THE TIMBER PROBLEM

Heating Roman buildings was a priority for Roman architects, and one way to do this was with a hypocaust. This was an ingenious system that circulated hot air from furnaces underneath floors and through hollow walls. The fundamental problem with hypocausts, however, was that they relied on wood to fuel the furnaces – a lot of it. This particular form of Roman heating was expensive, time-consuming and labour-intensive. To heat a large villa would require more than forty-eight cubic feet of wood every two days. Over the course of an entire year, that's an awful lot of trees.

Timber was, however, fundamental to the existence of the Roman empire in other ways too. The largest trees were crucial for the construction of houses, temples and other large public buildings; of merchant and naval ships; of army barracks and siege weapons; and they formed part of defensive walls, bridges and aqueducts. Smaller timbers were used everywhere, in construction projects of almost any type imaginable.

Wood was also crucial as fuel for industry. Any form of trade or craft that needed heat – from the creation of the simplest of pots to the most complex golden necklace or iron harness for a horse – needed enormous supplies of timber. Areas around locations used for mining and metallurgy in particular became deforested.

The heating of houses with wood-burning furnaces for domestic use, therefore, competed with all sorts of activities that were integral to the foundations and future of Rome. As timber was consumed in and around Rome, so supplies had to be imported from further and further afield, raising the cost of this central raw material.

The result was that houses – even buildings with hypocausts

– were constructed in a way that optimized the heat of the sun. Far from being a modern innovation, solar power has its roots in ancient civilizations, one of which was Rome.

HEATING THE HOME

One reason for doing this in domestic houses was to maximize the power of the sun during the winter, in order to ensure that at least one area of a building could be as hot as was possible at the coldest time of the year. This was done by constructing a sheltered area within the house that faced south and therefore caught the sun's rays. During the winter months, the sun rises late, skids low over the horizon, and sets early; its period of reasonable solar strength is short-lived. Rooms were, therefore, built to harness this relatively brief period. We get a vivid sense of what this kind of room was like in a letter from Pliny the Younger:

> The house has a large drawing room, and also a second drawing room of smaller size, which has one window facing the rising sun, and another facing the setting sun... This arrangement makes the room quite hot; it serves as a winter retreat.

Another way of making the most of the sun's energy in domestic buildings was to build floors in a such a way that the heat of the sun was retained. Marcus Cetius Faventinus, an architect working in the third to fourth century CE, explained in his manual *De Diversis Fabricis Architectonicae* how to do so:

> Excavate the earth to a depth of 2 foot, ram it down and put in rubble or a pavement of earthenware. Then gather cinders and trample them into a thick mass, and apply a layer containing a mixture of dark sand, ashes and lime, and 6 inches in thickness. The surface of this, brought to

the level with a square, gives the appearance of a black
pavement. So in winter time it does not absorb cold;
and its warmth will please your serving-men even when
barefoot.

'It will, too,' Faventinus adds, 'be the sort of pavement [or
floor] that will absorb in a moment the liquids spilt at drinking
parties.'

Pliny the Younger (61–c.113 CE)

A Roman author, administrator, lawyer and politician,
whose letters offer a unique glimpse into Roman life.
Achieving the rank of consul in 100 CE, he also headed
both the military treasury and senatorial treasury. Aged
thirty-nine, he began to publish collections of his private
letters – nine volumes in total. They cover a range of
topics from domestic news to moral discussions, his literary life and general advice.

BATHING AND SUN OVENS

The Romans also harnessed solar power to create a summery
space in their bathhouses for lounging, lizard-like, in the sun.
As with the sheltered areas in domestic homes, these structures
tended to be built facing south – or occasionally south-west – to
best capture the sun as it passed through the sky from its zenith
at noon to its setting on the western horizon. This heat from the
sun set the Roman habit of bathing between midday and evening,
a pattern of behaviour that the first-century BCE architect and
author Vitruvius described as 'fixed'.

Vitruvius (c.80–after 15 BCE)

An architect, engineer and author. His only surviving work is the ten-volume *De Architectura*, a handbook for Roman architects. Heavily influenced by Greek knowledge, it covers innumerable aspects of civil and military architecture and landscape design, and also describes historical events. Often known as the 'first architect', he was not actually the first; but he *was* the first to write about his area of expertise. His book was lost to history until a copy was discovered in the library of the monastery of St Gall in Switzerland in 1414. It went on to profoundly influence the Renaissance.

There is significant evidence that public baths were designed to incorporate the additional feature of window openings in the walls that could be glazed, which would have created a greenhouse effect – with the heat of the light coming into the building and then being trapped by the glass. Roman glazing first appeared during the reign of Augustus (27 BCE–14 CE), and was mounted in frames made of wood, stone or metal. The best archaeological evidence for this glazing of bathhouse windows comes from Herculaneum and Pompeii: the glass in the *caldarium* (the room with a hot plunge bath) of the suburban baths at Herculaneum was blown out by the impact of the volcanic flow from the eruption of Vesuvius in 79 CE and was scattered on the floor; elsewhere in the towns, window glass in various bathhouses was preserved *in situ*.

This principle of harnessing the sun's strength was taken to the extreme in some private residences, in an area known as the *heliocaminus* (or 'sun oven'). This room projected out from the main building and faced south to catch the full strength of the sun; it was nothing less than an amphitheatre for sunbathing.

Only tantalizing glimpses of such rooms appear in the literature. The third-century jurist Ulpian heard a case in which a man described how his neighbour had built an extension onto his house which blocked the sun from the plaintiff's sunroom. In his ruling, Ulpian was careful to distinguish between the light provided by the sun (*lumen*) and the heat it provided (*sol*). Ulpian decided that if any object obstructed the sun's heat where it was not needed, no action was granted; but if it was placed so as to block the sun's heat where it was essential – such as a *heliocaminus* – then the offending structure would have to go, as it would be 'in violation of the... right to the sun'. His decision was deemed sufficiently important to be written down in the sixth-century *Digest of Justinian*, evidence that litigation regarding solar access continued right up until the end of the Roman empire.

LIGHT

Roman architects also harnessed the sun for its light-giving power, and nowhere is this more intriguing than in the Pantheon in Rome. This remarkable building that still stands today was completed during the reign of Hadrian (117–138 CE), the emperor who fixated more than any other on the way that buildings could be used to send a message to his citizens.

The exact purpose and workings of the Pantheon remain beyond our grasp, though its status as a temple is certainly suggested by its name: the Greek *pan*, meaning 'all', and *theos*, meaning 'gods'. Recent research has focused on its relationship to the sun. The building is a unique structure, constructed of several parts. The main body consists of an enormous circular room which is covered by a cast-concrete dome forty-three metres in diameter – the largest unreinforced masonry dome in the world, and an engineering wonder of the ancient world. At the centre of the dome is an oculus, or circular window, which lets light into the room below in a very controlled and limited way.

This room with its domed ceiling has a rectangular porch attached to the front, containing the main entrance – which, unusually for temples, that all tend to face east or west (or occasionally south), faces north. This means that the main body of the Pantheon *never* receives any direct sunlight, other than that which comes through the oculus as a contained and powerful beam.

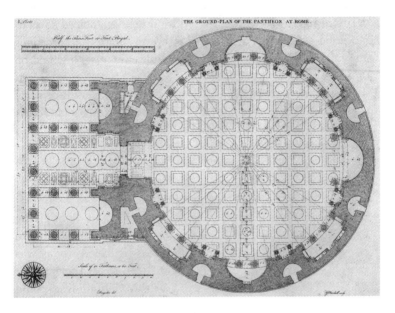

Plan of the Pantheon in Rome, seventeenth century

As the sun rises and sets and the days pass, therefore, the sun's beam, emanating from the centre of the heavenly dome, moves around the Pantheon's interior. Moreover, as the seasons go by and the sun's path in the sky changes, so the areas of the Pantheon that are lit by the sun's beam also change.

This much is known and understood, but little more. The Pantheon has been a Catholic church since the seventh century, and any markings which may have helped us understand its workings before that time have been lost.

There are, however, other ways in which the building itself offers clues to its function. As the sun moves through the sky, the beam of light from the oculus falls on notable parts of the building's interior construction. During the March and September equinoxes, when the centre of the sun is directly over the earth's equator, the beam falls just above the doorway that leads from the porch into the main circular room, where it shines through a grille. Most importantly, the entire doorway itself is bathed in light at solar noon on 21 April – the very date that tradition maintained Rome was founded by Romulus and his twin brother Remus in 753 BCE.

Historians have argued that one possible – though purely hypothetical – interpretation of this architectural detail is that a ritual was conducted at this exact time and on this exact day on an annual basis. Perhaps the emperor entered the Pantheon, bathed in sunlight with everything else in shade and with the sun appearing as a halo around his head – a visible representation that he was closest to heaven and the gods, and a striking confirmation of his divine power.

·11·
FISH

Roman mosaic of fish and ducks, from first century BCE

Fish are all about Roman luxury…

'PUTREFYING MATTER' VS FRESH FISH

Preserved fish – dried, smoked or, most commonly, salted – was widely accessible and widely consumed throughout the Roman world, and so too was processed fish in the form of *garum*, a type of fish sauce that was a by-product of the fish-salting process. *Garum* was traded throughout the empire, and for many years was so popular that it became a culinary symbol of being Roman – whether you were in Africa, Northumbria or central Asia. Fresh fish, on the other hand, was different: it was primarily a symbol of wealth, and sometimes of excessive wealth.

If you had limited income but no access to nets or lines yourself, some fresh fish was affordable, though not cheap. An expenditure account from Roman Egypt in the first century CE reveals that a small-sized fish cost the equivalent of two loaves of bread, or six eggs. And large and fresh fish were a prized commodity indeed. They fetched large sums of money at markets, and were a delicacy at the tables of the wealthy.

The *Colloquia of the Hermeneumata Pseudodositheana*, a collection of manuals written for ancient Romans and Greeks to get by in each other's languages – and one of the most important historical sources for understanding Roman daily life – makes the differentiation between preserved and fresh fish very clear. The preparation of a feast is described and the foodstuffs named: 'vegetables, good salt fish and fresh fish, meat, sweet wine, and chickens'. Note how only 'good' salt fish was permitted on such a special occasion, suggestive of the different levels of quality of preserved fish available, but that the 'fresh' fish is entitled to be there on account of its freshness alone.

So prized was fresh fish within Roman society that it was

sent as gifts to curry favour. In a letter written in the Arsinoites province in Egypt and dated 7 January 108 CE, an ex-soldier named Lucius Bellenus Gemellus asks his son to buy fish and send it to an official he is trying to influence – or, in Lucius's words, 'as we want to make use of him'. The word for 'fish' used in the letter is important – it is *ichthydion*, a Greek term used specifically for fresh fish. Similarly, the poet Martial records with a wry smile how a social climber named Papylus sent red mullets and oysters as gifts to impress his peers, but left himself only the tail of a *lacertus* – a small and undesirable lizard-fish – for his own supper; in other words, he was prepared to sacrifice his own culinary pleasures in order to forward his political career.

The emphasis placed on freshness is also revealed in mosaics discovered in the ruins of Pompeii, depicting fish laid out in their 'whole' state prior to cooking, and so fresh they appear to have just been caught, the bountiful gifts of plenty of an opulent household.

FISH PONDS

Fresh fish became so important as a status symbol that the Romans designed and built special ponds in which to farm them. If access to fresh fish was a measure of a certain status, as it revealed relationships with local tradesmen secured through favour and expense, then guaranteed regular access to fresh fish for yourself and your guests – without having to leave your property – was the next step up.

There is some evidence that ponds were also used as business ventures, producing sought-after fish for wealthy clients, and several very large examples of fish ponds have survived, the largest known being in Torre Astura near Anzio, a coastal city just south of Rome. This pond is 15,000 square metres, the size of two football pitches. The majority of the evidence, however, both archaeological and literary, is of private fish ponds custom-designed and constructed exclusively for wealthy patrons – and they are impressive engineering achievements.

Some are directly cut out from seaside rocks, but more often they were built away from the sea and made watertight using a special type of cement that set underwater. Fish ponds also required channels and sluices to keep the water moving, in order to keep the fish healthy, and they were often divided into sections to keep apart different species, as well as fish at different stages of growth. The ponds were often built in curious shapes – lozenges, circles and rectangles – to be viewed from balconies above and appreciated for their aesthetics. The author and philosopher Seneca tells us that some were even built inside banqueting rooms, as one particular type of fish – the mullet – could not be considered fresh unless it was brought to the table alive and dispatched there. Of course, all of this required a great deal of money, and some of the rarest of expertise. The Roman scholar Varro was wryly clear of the expense entailed in constructing artificial fish ponds: 'For in the first place they are built at great cost, in the second place they are stocked at great cost, and in the third place they are kept up at great cost.'

Although there is evidence of the Romans keeping a wide variety of fish in their ponds, by far the most popular were those known as *murenae* – a word that referred to all eel-like creatures, including *anguillae* (common eels), *congri* (conger eels), morays and lampreys. Eels were ideal for fish ponds because they could adapt to a wide range of salinity, grow very large and be kept in very high densities, unlike other fish.

Unusual home-raised fish became unusually valuable. Pliny the Elder tells us that a single mullet once sold for 8,000 sesterces, and according to the imperial biographer Suetonius, the emperor Tiberius was disgusted that three such fish went for 30,000 sesterces, more than thirty times the annual salary of an ordinary Roman legionary. Lucius Licinius Lucullus, who was consul in 74 BCE and whose builders and engineers dug through a mountain to get water to the fish ponds on his estate near Naples, had such a large stock of unusual fish that they sold for 4 million sesterces on his death.

Live fish even became pets of the wealthy, a source of delight and entertainment beyond the plate. Cicero inevitably politicized the phenomenon in a letter to his friend Atticus (c.110–32 BCE), dubbing the upper class '*piscinarii*' ('fish fanciers' or 'fish-ponders') and claiming that fish pond owners spent far too much time caring about their *piscinae* when they should be showing concern for the Roman republic.

Other writers seized the opportunity for ridicule. Martial, the Roman poet from Hispania (modern Spain), spoke of how 'delicate lampreys swim up to their master; delicious mullet obey the call of the keeper, and the old carp come forth at the sound of his voice'; and Pliny the Elder recorded how Drusus's wife gave earrings to her favourite eel and how the consul and orator Hortensius wept when his favourite moray died – though Pliny was never one to let the truth get in the way of a good story.

Hortensius (114–50 BCE)

Quintus Hortensius Hortalus was a distinguished advocate and politician, becoming consul in 69 BCE. Almost no detail of his speeches survives, but the force of his oratory is apparent in numerous descriptions of him, and his success is evident in the immense wealth he acquired. In later life he was a dedicated gourmand. He was the first to keep wild boars for the table and to serve peacocks.

BOOKS ON FISH

So popular were fish and fish-eating among the wealthy that authors including some of the greatest names in Roman literature – Oppian, Lucretius, Pliny, Athenaeus and Ovid among them – began to write about fish. Pliny noted that, up until his time, no fewer than eighteen authors had written treatises on fish. Books on fish were a notable and curious literary characteristic of the early empire – luxuries in themselves, written to entertain their knowledgeable and wealthy fish-loving readers.

The authors focused not only on descriptions of fish but also advice on how to catch them and which were the best for eating. A fine example comes from the writings of the well-travelled writer Apuleius (c.124–c.170 CE). Writing for the elite fish-connoisseur, his knowledge of the subject was based on ancient wisdom originally gathered for a Macedonian, or possibly Epirote, court:

> How superior to all is the sea weasel [moray] of Clipea, the 'mice' are at Aenos, the rough oysters are fullest at Abydos. The scallop is of Mytilene, and the 'pig' of Ambracia near Charadrum. The sea bream at Brundisium is good; take it, if it is large. Know that the best little boar-fish [grunt fish] is prime at Tarentum; you should buy the elops at Surrenti and the glaucus near Cumae. What? Have I passed up the parrotfish, nearly the brain of supreme Jupiter (It is caught in the country of Nestor and is big and good), and the black-tail, the 'thrush', the blackbird and the sea ghost. Octopus of Corcyra, the fat skull-fish, the purple fish, the murriculi, the murex and also the sea urchins are sweet.

Such solid advice was mixed with fantastical tales of sea creatures. Pliny in particular, who had commanded a Roman fleet and spent much time at sea, enjoyed a good maritime story, even if there was a rational explanation. He devoted two entire books (numbers 9 and 32) of his 10-volume, 37-book *Naturalis Historia* to the subject of marine animals, including a description of a 'polyp' with such extended limbs that it could not pass through the Straits of Gibraltar, and another of a fish of such size that people used its jawbones for doorways and its bones for roof beams. He subsequently revealed, rather whimsically, that the 'polyp' was an alga and the enormous fish a whale.

·12·

BENCHES

The *schola* tomb of the priestess Mamia in Pompeii, c.63 BCE–14 CE

Benches are all about Roman public service…

POMPEII'S BENCHES

Roman cities were scattered with public benches – and archaeological work in Pompeii has uncovered a huge variety of public
seating. Outside the gates of this former ancient city are nine
tombs built to honour high-ranking city benefactors, known as
'*schola* tombs'. Semi-circular in shape, they are benches built as
a public service, slightly raised to give a good view of passing
traffic and to offer a place of rest. Seats and seated areas are
often associated with Roman tombs, but here the bench itself
is the funerary monument. These benches are large – the tomb
of Mamia near the Porta di Ercolano is 6.6 metres long – and
would have been places to socialize, where one could sit with
others to enjoy the passing bustle of the city while pondering
the memory of the deceased; they are resting places fashioned
from a place of rest. The worn steps up to Mamia's tomb are
testament to just how popular such a place was among the
locals and visitors to Pompeii.

Inside the city are benches that are not tombs but which were
similarly built to pass the time. A recent survey of the accessible
streets of Pompeii (bear in mind that 30 per cent of the city still
remains buried) revealed no fewer than 100 benches associated
with 69 different properties – benches where people would sit to
pass the time of day were nothing less than an urban phenomenon here.

These benches range in size from one to ten metres long,
and are all intentionally built in street-side locations: sometimes flush against the front of a property; sometimes in a
corner, where one building juts out slightly further than
another; sometimes slightly recessed into a building, but

facing the street. As a general rule they are well-built with good craftsmanship, and are constructed from high-quality brick and stone in order to be long-lasting. They would have been relatively expensive to build and yet they are found all over the city.

Analysis of the location of the benches in relation to the sun has suggested that they were built with the sitter's comfort in mind: in shade through the hottest time of the day, and only directly in sunlight with the warm evening sun. There is also a notable hotspot along the streets between the theatres and the amphitheatre, where pedestrian traffic would have been greatest. These benches are evidence of the buildings' owners wanting to make an impression – providing places for people to sit and pass the time – just as the city's elite who built those *schola* tombs just outside the city's gates were providing a small but significant public service for the weary and the chatty.

ENTERTAINMENT

Benches in theatres and amphitheatres were another significant aspect of Roman society linked to public service, and are best explored through the magnificent Colosseum, Rome's enormous amphitheatre that could seat around 50,000 spectators. Seating was provided by wooden planks on marble benches for all but the most elite. Senators were allowed a type of folding stool known as a *sella curulis*, while the emperor would have sat or reclined on a larger ceremonial chair without a back – akin to a small bench for two – known as a *bisellium*.

Entrance to the Colosseum was free, though a clever system existed to funnel the spectators to the correct place once they were in the stadium. The seating was allocated according to strict social status divisions, taking into account property ownership, financial means, profession, religious affiliation and gender.

Various sources suggest that this came about when, at an unknown date, a law was passed under Augustus (ruled 27 BCE–14 CE) called the *Lex Julia Theatralis*, which sought to impose the emperor's rigid view of an orderly hierarchical Roman society upon the audiences at public events. Previously, the social elite – the *senatores* and the *equites* – were seated separately from the rest of the spectators; but now lines were drawn elsewhere throughout society. The Roman historian Suetonius wrote approvingly of these changes, noting how Augustus ended the 'wholly confused and lax way of watching shows and introduced order'.

Although the exact system of ticketing or tokens is unknown, the archaeological evidence shows that the building would at one time have been surrounded by a series of bollards or posts, each with a ring on top to hold chain or rope and with grooves for wooden barriers. These would have been set up to funnel spectators to the correct entrance, according to their social standing. We also know a little about the internal arrangements of the benches in the Colosseum, from references in writing and even inscriptions on the surviving stairs and benches marking them out for certain sections of society. At the north and south ends, at a height that gave the best view, were boxes set aside for the emperor himself and the Vestal Virgins. Flanking these, and therefore visibly close to the emperor, were areas for the social and political elite of the senatorial class; above them sat the *equites*, the influential business class; and higher up still was an area for ordinary Roman citizens, the plebeians. Other specific areas were provided for particular types of people: boys with their tutors, soldiers on leave, foreign dignitaries, scribes, heralds and priests. During the reign of Domitian, between 81 and 96 CE, another gallery was built at the very top for the common poor, where slaves and women of all ranks (who Augustus had insisted on keeping separate from the men) could watch but only from a standing position. These women and slaves did not even get a bench.

Vestal Virgins

Priestesses of Vesta, the goddess of the hearth. Chosen between the ages of six and ten by the *pontifex maximus* – the chief high priest of the College of Pontiffs – they served for thirty years, having to remain virgins, after which they were permitted to marry. The role came with certain perks – not least emancipation from their father's rule and permission to own their own property – but if they broke their vow of chastity, they would be buried alive.

The tiers of benches in the Colosseum were divided into sections, which were themselves then subdivided into rows, with marks made in the marble outlining the extent of each seat. Not only was providing seating for entertainment a public service; so too, in Augustus's mind, was organizing it in a way that reflected Roman society. Exactly what was thought of this seating system is unknown, but it certainly caused a problem for love-struck Roman youths. The first-century BCE poet Propertius recalled how he had fallen in love, but after the new laws could no longer be so carefree with his ogling of women. He warned himself that there would be 'no more cruising at festival time in the Forum', and that, when at the Colosseum, he had to 'beware that thou bend not thy neck awry to gaze at the theatre's topmost ring'. It would seem that his social standing gave him a bench from which to view the games – but that wasn't necessarily what he was interested in.

ROMAN GOVERNMENT

Benches were also significant as a symbol of public service at the very heart of the Roman government – in the Curia, the building in the Forum where the Senate usually met to debate and pass laws.

The Senate

The Senate was an unelected body responsible for the health of the empire. It controlled the treasury, voted on new legislation, established policy and supervised the administration of provinces. Although its influence rose and fell over time, it was ever-present in Roman history and had been so from the very beginning: at some point between 753 and 716 BCE, the first Roman king, Romulus, founded an advisory council of 100 men, which became the Senate.

The Curia was specifically designed for these meetings. The way that the building worked was similar to the British House of Commons. Rectangular in shape, the senators sat opposite each other on tiers of wooden benches on either long side of the chamber, which was divided by a central aisle. Particular positions on the benches were not allocated to individuals, though spaces on the front benches were reserved for former magistrates, meaning that those who sat at the back were less important – just as backbenchers are less important in today's House of Commons than 'frontbench' MPs.

If all of the senators came at one time – a figure which rose from 300 up to around 900 during Caesar's dictatorship and 1,000 under the First Triumvirate (when Rome was ruled by an alliance of Caesar, Crassus and Pompey) – there was insufficient bench space for all those eligible to sit in Senate, just as there is insufficient space on the benches of the House of Commons for all MPs. This meant that on important occasions, when the majority of the senators were present, the most junior members would often have to stand; it has been suggested that this was perhaps one of the reasons that these people were known as *pedarii* ('footmen').

The significance of benches in the day-to-day running of the Roman government extended to the representatives of the ordinary citizens of Rome – the *tribuni plebis* ('tribunes of the people'), who were also provided with benches from which they could exercise their power. The branch of government they belonged to, which was open to plebeians, was set up in 493 BCE as a check on the power of the unelected senators and magistrates. Tribunes could convene the plebeian assembly and propose their own legislation, but most importantly they could veto almost any act of legislation passed by the Senate or a magistrate of any kind.

To enforce this, the tribunes (in theory at least) had the power to inflict punishment – even the death penalty – on any magistrate who defied their veto. These powers, however, came with certain restrictions. Notably that tribunes had to make themselves available to the people at any time of day or night. They could not be away from home for a single night and had to leave their door open. The idea behind this was that the tribune could be reached in an emergency to discharge one very specific duty: the *ius auxilii* – the 'right to help'. This gave the tribunes the right to assist a plebeian wronged by an official act of a patrician magistrate.

To discharge their public service during the day, the tribunes were provided with benches in two very significant locations. The first was outside the entrance to the Curia, where they could keep an eye on the proceedings of the Senate but also be accessible to the public. The second was near the Tarpeian Rock, where public executions were carried out. These benches, therefore, were a type of civic-service contact point and help desk for ordinary people. They were also a location for indirect political dissent. In 45 BCE, when Caesar returned to Rome at the successful conclusion of his civil war against Pompey, he processed in a triumph through the streets of Rome. When he passed the tribune's benches, one tribune, Pontius Aquila, refused to stand, instead continuing to sit on his seat of power. Caesar was furious at this display of independence – a direct challenge to his Roman *dignitas* (dignity and prestige). He took no further action, but according to Suetonius he could not help but engage in some verbal sparring. 'Come then, Aquila,' he cried, 'take back the republic from me, you tribune.' And for several days after this, Caesar would not make any promise without adding: 'That is, if Pontius Aquila will allow me.'

·13·

WEAVING

Mosaic of Hercules dressed as a woman holding a distaff and spindle, used for spinning, and Omphale dressed as Hercules, third century CE

Weaving is all about Roman female self-expression...

WOMEN'S SKILLS

Working with wool (known in Latin as *lanificium*) through spinning and weaving, mending and sewing – alongside cooking, cleaning, water-carrying and child-minding – was a fundamental part of the education of Roman girls, which aimed to equip them to be able to manage households. Women of all social levels were involved in weaving: maids might impress mistresses with their skills; slave girls worked as dressmakers and wool-workers; and married women made homespun garments (or, if they were rich, oversaw others working with fabric). The Roman writer Varro considered that girls should learn embroidery in order that they might learn discernment in home furnishings – weaving in this sense was connected to taste and refinement. Needlework was also a leisure-time pursuit for women of high social status. Propertius described his muse Cynthia staying awake and weaving 'purple threads'.

While by the first century BCE ready-made fabrics were available to buy for those able to afford them, female facility with wool-working was one of the skills that was traditionally prized among brides. In traditional Roman weddings, according to the Greek author Plutarch, 'When they lead in the bride, they spread a fleece beneath her; she herself brings with her a distaff and her spindle and wreaths her husband's door with wool.' These instruments of weaving and spinning represented the wife's worth as a contributor to the household economy.

Most Roman garments were made of wool or linen, and great care was taken with sheep in order to preserve the quality of their fleece, including dressing flocks in leather jackets. The process of turning fleece into fabric was multi-layered: starting with the washing of the fleece, the combing of the wool and the separating of the fibres. It was then dyed before being spun and woven, normally by using one of two types of loom: warp-weighted and two-beam.

Propertius (c.50–c.15 BCE)

An important Latin poet who produced four books of *Elegies* during the reign of Augustus, Sextus Propertius was friends with Gallus and Virgil. His first book of love elegies in 25 BCE featured 'Cynthia', based on an older woman of his acquaintance who became his muse.

— EMPRESS LIVIA'S HOMESPUN DRESSES —

Weaving was particularly important to Roman women because it provided them with a means of self-expression and allowed them to achieve a degree of independence and power. The evidence for this is fleeting and fragmentary, but one of the best surviving examples comes from Suetonius's *Life of Augustus*. In it, we are told that the women of Augustus's family, including his wife Livia, were involved in making his clothes:

> Except on special occasions he wore common clothes for the house, made by his sister, wife, daughter or granddaughters; his togas were neither close nor full, his purple stripe neither narrow nor broad, and his shoes somewhat high-soled, to make him look taller than he really was. But he always kept shoes and clothing to wear in public ready in his room for sudden and unexpected occasions.

It is most likely that, rather than making the clothes themselves, Livia and the other family members oversaw the work of skilled servants within the household. Nevertheless, the choice of homespun garments made by women was an important way of expressing simple tastes for an emperor who was famed for his loathing of extravagance.

Livia avoided the criticisms levelled at other empresses about the luxuriance of their wardrobes, which may suggest that she too wore homespun clothing. In this way, she would have conformed to the model of a modest wife – an ideal *matrona* – as proposed by the philosopher and author Seneca in the first century CE. If she 'wants to be safe from the lust of a seducer' he wrote, she 'must go out dressed up only so far as to avoid unkemptness'. Weaving as a skill associated with feminine virtue was therefore part of the way in which Augustus and Livia represented themselves as the exemplary imperial couple.

PHILOMELA'S TAPESTRY

One of the clearest examples of weaving used as a form of female self-expression can be found in the Latin retelling for Roman audiences of Ovid's *Metamorphoses*, which contains the tragic story of Philomela, one of the daughters of Pandion I, King of Athens. In the myth, Philomela is raped by Tereus – King of Thrace and husband of her sister, Procne – and then mutilated, having her tongue cut out so that she cannot speak about the crime. So she turns to weaving in order to communicate the horrors perpetrated upon her, as described in Ovid's narrative poem:

> The sun god circles
> through twelve constellations. A year goes by.
> What can Philomela do? There is a guard
> to keep her from escaping, and the walls
> of the place where she is held are thick,

made out of solid rock. Her speechless lips
can provide no details of what happened.
But pain promotes great ingenuity,
and when times are bad one grows resourceful.
With great skill she pulls thread into a warp
on a barbarian loom, and, by weaving
patterns of purple on a white background,
she depicts the crime. Once she is finished,
she entrusts the weaving to a servant,
asking her with gestures to present it
to the queen, her mistress, and the servant,
as requested, carries it to Procne,
not knowing what the woven work contains.
The wife of the savage tyrant unfolds
the tapestry and, looking at it, reads
her sister's dreadful fate. She says nothing.
It is amazing she can keep so quiet,
but grief prevents her speech. Her tongue seeks out
words which might be adequate to express
her murderous rage, but cannot find them.
With no time to weep, she rushes ahead,
so totally intent on her revenge,
she no longer separates right from wrong.

On reading her sister's stitched testimony of the monstrous treatment at the hands of Tereus, Procne seeks revenge on her husband by murdering their son, Itys, dismembering his body and serving it up to her husband as a banquet. After he has finished, Procne and her sister present him with the head of his son as evidence that he has just consumed his own offspring. In a thunderous rage, Tereus pursues the two sisters with the intention of killing them for their deadly deeds, but as they escape the pair plea to the gods and are transformed into birds: in Ovid's version he does not specify, but in the traditional mythology Procne becomes a nightingale, and Philomela a swallow.

PENELOPE AMONG HER SUITORS

Another Greek myth that found itself translated for a Roman audience – and which also illustrates how the act of weaving might empower women – comes from Homer's *Odyssey* (composed in the eighth century BCE) and features the character Penelope, the faithful wife of Odysseus, the hero of Homer's epic work.

The narrative about Penelope takes place during the long absence of her husband, who is away for some twenty years fighting in the Trojan War. During this period, Penelope is the model of wifely fidelity, despite more than one hundred suitors trying to claim her hand in marriage. One of the ruses she employs to delay these romantic advances is to say that she is weaving a funeral shroud for her father-in-law Laertes, and that only when she has finished will she make herself available to marry. Her trick over a three-year period is to unpick at night all the stitching she completed during the day, and thus she is able to avoid the unwanted advances of her various male suitors. She is eventually betrayed by a female slave, who reveals her trickery to the men.

The *Odyssey*

A major Greek epic poem by the literary giant Homer. It was in part a sequel to his other major work, the *Iliad*, and follows the adventures of the Greek hero Odysseus (Ulysses to the Romans) as he journeys home after the fall of Troy. The work had a profound influence on Western literary traditions – not least the Romans – and many of the themes and stories are retold by Latin authors.

The steadfastness of Penelope as an honourable wife is a recurrent theme in Latin literature, and she crops up in the work of authors such as Ovid, Plautus, Martial, Statius, Horace and Propertius. In Book I of Ovid's *Tristia*, he celebrates her 'fame', while in his epistolary work *Heroides* he presents a letter of complaint written in the name of Penelope to her husband, pondering whether or not she should wait for him. It is in Propertius's love elegies, however, that we receive an account of Penelope's craftiness as a weaver.

In this episode, she is making the funeral shroud of her very elderly father-in-law, a depiction that presents an image not only of a virtuous wife – chiming with the representations of weaving – but also of a woman occupied in an honourable pursuit:

> Penelope was able to live un-touched for twenty years, a woman worthy of so many suitors. She was able to evade marriage by cunning weaving, cleverly unravelling the day's weft by night: and though she never hoped to see Ulysses again, she stayed, growing old, waiting for his return.

·14·
FATTENING

Vitellio

The emperor Vitellius, depicted in an Italian Renaissance bronze plaque from the sixteenth century, on display in the Bargello Museum, Florence

Fattening is all about the Roman way of life...

FAT MICE

The careful fattening of certain animals to eat was a striking characteristic of Roman cuisine from the middle of the Roman republic, around 250 BCE, and for the first two centuries of the empire, up to around 250 CE. Various animals were fattened, including thrushes, snails, and fish, but most notable in the sources are dormice.

Dormice were everywhere in the ancient world, and the Romans' fascination with them is an important counter to their obsession with exotic creatures (see p. 34). The dormouse was common, easy to breed, cheap to purchase and native to Italy. At the same time that wealthy gourmands acquired an appetite for the most exotic of animals, and the choicest of animal parts were consumed as delicacies (not least flamingo tongues and camel heels), the dormouse remained a firm favourite of the Roman palate. There was, however, one important characteristic of the type of dormouse favoured by the Romans – it had been deliberately fattened.

There is both literary and archaeological evidence for this process. The literary evidence includes a passage from the scholar Varro, who wrote of how dormice could be fattened in outdoor pens that contained acorn-producing trees and hollows in the ground where the sated mice could breed. Having discussed the breeding of snails – another Roman comestible – in a section of his *Res Rustica* that deals with agriculture, Varro explains that:

> The place for dormice is built on a different plan, as the ground is surrounded not by water but by a wall, which is

covered on the inside with smooth stone or plaster over the whole surface, so that they cannot creep out of it. In this place there should be small nut-bearing trees; when they are not bearing, acorns and chestnuts should be thrown inside the walls for them to glut themselves with. They should have rather roomy caves built for them in which they can bring forth their young; and the supply of water should be small, as they do not use much of it, but prefer a dry place.

He continues:

They are fattened in jars, which many people keep even inside the villa. The potters make these jars in a very different form from other jars, as they run channels along the sides and make a hollow for holding the food. In such a jar acorns, walnuts or chestnuts are placed; and when a cover is placed over the jars they grow fat in the dark.

Examples of these fattening pots can be found among the archaeological evidence in the form of uniquely designed terracotta jars known as *dolia*. These sealable jars restricted the mice's movements while giving them easy access to grains and nuts provided by the owner. They are identifiable by the perforated walls that would have allowed the mice to breathe, and by a type of spiral run on the inside to help the pots resemble a burrow. A lid kept the interior in darkness, an important design feature, because the Romans knew that dormice store fat before they hibernate. Remarkably, nine such jars have survived the centuries to be discovered by archaeologists – five of which are in the collections of the National Archaeological Museum of Naples.

It is not clear whether or not these jars were part of a two-stage fattening process carried out by professional breeders, in which the dormice were first kept outside in a deliberately designed enclosure before being placed in jars – or indeed whether the jars represent a type of DIY mouse-fattening kit for the everyday mouse-hungry Roman.

WHY DORMICE?

The fascination with fattened dormice was linked to the display of wealth and the giving of gifts. Small animals like dormice and thrushes are particularly difficult to fatten – unlike, for example, pigs; it takes relatively more food and time to fatten a smaller animal than a large one. And so, to the Romans, these were not simply rodents engorged to feed the poor, but rather choice foodstuffs intended to pleasure and impress. A nicely fattened dormouse was a demonstration of time and money spent in its preparation for the table – and to be seen to eat such a delicacy, and to offer it to guests, was to demonstrate social or economic status. So sought-after were they that attempts to prohibit their eating by a sumptuary law promulgated in 115 BCE proved ineffectual.

Something of the lavish nature of this Roman delicacy is conveyed by the details of its preparation. When ready for consuming, the plump dormouse would be rolled in honey and poppy seeds before being roasted or braised. To heap fattening upon fattening, they could also be mouth-wateringly stuffed with bacon, fruit and spices. A recipe from the period that survives in the collection *Apicius* (or *De Re Coquinaria*) recommends that the dormouse is 'stuffed with a forcemeat of pork and small pieces of dormouse meat trimmings, all pounded with pepper, nuts... [and] broth'. Then, it instructs, one should: 'Put the dormouse thus stuffed in an earthen casserole, roast it in the oven, or boil it in the stock pot.'

When the fattened dormouse was finally served, the moment might be recorded for posterity. The soldier and historian Ammianus Marcellinus (c.330–c.400 CE) wrote that, at some banquets:

the scales are even called for, in order to weigh the fish, birds and dormice that are served, whose great size they recommend again and again, as hitherto unexampled, often repeating it to the weariness of those present, especially when thirty secretaries stand near by, with pen-cases and small tablets, recording these same items, so that the only thing lacking seems to be a schoolmaster.

In situations like this, the Romans were making certain that the fattened mice were given the attention for which they were bred. The fact that we still know about the Roman appreciation of a good fat dormouse is telling that *they* wanted everyone to know about it.

FAT PEOPLE

The Roman view of fat *people*, however was not so straightforward. Literary references suggest that fatness was frowned upon.

The value of a regimented, healthy type of lifestyle was appreciated by Roman medics for various reasons. Some believed that obesity led to sterility. They believed that in the process of fattening, blood was transformed into fat instead of menstrual blood for women and semen for men. The Roman medical writer Galen (130–c.210 CE) believed that a large belly was a sign of a malformed spirit; the educator and rhetorician Quintilian (c.35–c.100 CE) advised the would-be orator to reduce body fat in order to remain healthy and robust; and Plutarch (c.46–120 CE) drew a direct link between obesity and public service, asking: 'What use can the state turn a man's body to, when all between throat and groin is taken up by the belly?'

This view is linked to the Roman appreciation of discipline and moderation, two traits that were best encapsulated by Caesar, who was known and celebrated for his slim physique, clearly reflected in his image on coins, in which he is all sharp lines, tight skin, clearly defined chin, nose and cheekbones.

Denarius coin depicting Julius Caesar, 44 BCE

An interesting example at the opposite end of this scale was the emperor Vitellius (15–69 CE), who was publicly murdered on the Gemonian Stairs in the Forum on 22 December 69 CE after a chaotic rule of just eight months.

Gemonian Stairs

A famous flight of stairs built some time during the rule of Tiberius - between 14 and 37 CE - they were located in the centre of the ancient city of Rome, leading from the Capitoline Hill down to the Roman Forum. They were nicknamed the 'Stairs of Mourning' because they were associated with executions. Those condemned to death might be strangled and then their bodies thrown down the stairs; other corpses were simply dumped there to be displayed as a grisly warning, and left to rot.

The historian Suetonius recorded how Vitellius was mocked at his death for his lameness, flushed face and obese stomach:

> All along the Sacred Way he was greeted with mockery and abuse, his head held back by the hair, as is common with criminals, and even the point of a sword placed under his chin, so that he could not look down but must let his face be seen. Some pelted him with dung and ordure, others called him incendiary and glutton, and some of the mob even taunted him with his bodily defects. He was in fact abnormally tall, with a face usually flushed from hard drinking, a huge belly, and one thigh crippled from being struck once upon a time by a four-horse chariot, when he was in attendance on Gaius as he was driving. At last on the Stairs of Wailing he was tortured for a long time and then dispatched and dragged off with a hook to the Tiber.

Vitellius's gluttony achieved considerable notice during his life as well. From the accounts that have survived, one is left in no doubt that his obesity played a significant part in the contemporary justification of his execution – a symbol of the greed, excess and lack of self-control that had defined his reign as it surely defined him; his fatness became a way of attacking him politically. With tongue in cheek, perhaps, Suetonius described how Vitellius would snatch meat from sacrificial altars to satisfy his hunger, and noted how such a lack of control was visible in other aspects of his rule, not least how he would kill or torture at 'the slightest pretext'.

Another historian, Cassius Dio (155–235 CE), linked this lack of control to money. He commented that 'addicted as he was to luxury and licentiousness, [Vitellius] no longer cared for anything else either human or divine' and that, once he became emperor, 'his wantonness only increased, and he was squandering money most of the day and night alike'.

·15·

SHOPPING

Relief from the port city of Ostia depicting shopping. Note that the figure working at the stall is a woman

Shopping is all about the underbelly of Roman society...

Towns and cities throughout the Roman world teemed with retailers of varying sorts, from simple food-sellers to luxury markets where the wealthy would bid for prized products for their opulent dinner tables, and bankers stood to hand, ready to supply the necessary credit. As the empire extended, trade routes brought into the capital city an expanding range of goods and commodities. Permanent shops thronged arcades and porticoes, and spilled over onto the streets. Alongside these shops appeared temporary stalls, which popped up on an ad hoc basis at key events, and itinerant pedlars and hawkers plied their wares across the city, often door-to-door. At one point, Rome was apparently so overcrowded with retailers of varying kinds that the poet Martial described the city as one big shop. And within this heady world of commerce, if we look carefully, we can find the underbelly of Roman society.

DISHONEST SHOPKEEPERS

Commerce within the ancient world was often seen as disreputable and in need of control. While many of the sources that disparage shopkeepers are elite and satirical, we are nonetheless presented with a rich seam of material that represents retailers as unreasonably pushy, on the make, and dishonest.

One of the best surviving examples occurs in a poem by the third-century BCE Alexandrian poet Herodas. It features a woman named Metro and a couple of her friends who visit a shoe shop owned by a man named Kerdon, fittingly nicknamed 'Mr Profiteer'. As soon as the women arrive at the shop, a bench is brought out for them to sit on, and they are presented with every pair of footwear on the premises – from sandals and slippers to boots and flats – all of which are accompanied by a sales pitch that mixes hyperbole about materials, design and fashion with a personal sob story from the shopkeeper about needing to feed so many mouths. Kerdon's salesmanship makes use of every trick in the book. Asking his servant to bring out all the 'shoecases', he implores his customers:

> soothly, dames, must ye have arms well laden ere ye go home. Ye shall descern: here are all these kinds: Sicyonian, little Ambracians, Nossians, Chians, parrots, hemps, Baucises, slippers, Ionian buttoned, hop-on-nights, ankle-tops, crabs, Argive sandals, scarlets, lads, stairs; say each what heart wish, that ye may know why women and dogs devour leather.

Shopkeepers were known for their sharp practices, and ancient texts are almost universal in their criticism of retailers and the poor quality of their goods. But writing found in Pompeii takes the shopkeepers' view and lauds the entrepreneurial spirit to be found there: one mosaic spells out the words 'Welcome profit!', while a graffito reads 'Profit is pleasure'. One fifth-century writer claimed that one disreputable practice was to keep eggs and onions in bowls of water to make them seem larger than they actually were. Far worse – though perhaps tongue in cheek – Galen claimed that some retailers used human flesh rather than pork in some of their dishes, and that many of their customers couldn't even tell the difference.

THE THREAT OF PEDLARS

Hawkers and street sellers were viewed as particularly suspect characters, especially when they visited the home to sell their wares and door-stepped the occupant without warning. Many ancient authors were worried about home visits and the sexual threat that these unexpected salesmen presented – especially when the women of the household might be bored with a humdrum life. Horace described the female poisoner Canidia as a woman who was loved by sailors and pedlars.

Ovid, on the other hand, felt that pedlars were disconcerting to men in other ways too, since they seemed to him to turn up when mistresses were in a mood for spending – which could result in a great expense to their male lovers.

Not all pedlars were men, however, and nor were all purchasers who were willing to be distracted female. A text by Petronius tells the story of an elderly woman vegetable seller who was simultaneously engaged in drumming up trade for a nearby brothel.

BARS AS AREAS OF DISREPUTE

In ancient Rome, rather than the city being subject to zoning – attempting to keep certain services and activities within particular quarters so that they were easier to control – retail outlets were spread across the metropolis, where they jostled with residences, temples and civic buildings. Bars in particular were not kept to specific areas – but, as a way of catching passing trade, they were set up in the busiest locations and at the inter-sections of roads. This can be discerned from the survival of stone counters which would once have stood in the bars, often with large serving vessels or jars built into the counter and stands behind.

An estimated 150 such establishments are thought to have existed in the city of Pompeii alone. One bar near to the amphitheatre with a small vineyard attached had painted on its exterior wall a phoenix, next to which was written the slogan 'The phoenix is happy and so can you be', presumably promising the delights of drinking. The entrance to another bar was hung with a bizarrely shaped lamp, which rather shocked archaeologists when they uncovered it. It features a small pygmy with an enormous phallus, almost the size of his body, with a second (smaller) member growing from the end of it. The figure carries a knife, almost as if he were about to sever this monstrous appendage. Attached to it are six bells, which presumably rang when customers entered and exited the bar.

Horace (65–8 BCE)

Quintus Horatius Flaccus, known simply as Horace, was one of the most significant Roman lyric poets of the Augustan era, his career coinciding with the transformation of Rome from republic to empire. Having fought in the republican army that was defeated at the Battle of Philippi in 42 BCE, he took an office under Augustus and was associated with the new regime. His major works include his *Satires*, *Epodes*, *Odes*, *Epistles* and *Ars Poetica*.

Bars were associated with suspicious activities: landlords on the make, goods of dubious quality, and as dens of iniquity where gambling, crime, sex and prostitution were rife. The Roman poet Horace wrote of the pleasures of 'the brothel and the greasy tavern', while the satirist Juvenal described the seedy lowlifes who populated the Roman port of Ostia – from murderers, thieves and coffin makers, to eunuch priests taking time off to get drunk in the town's bars.

Other paintings from Pompeii depict scenes of bar-life that are at once comic and parodying, but are nonetheless the nearest we can get to a visualization of café culture of the period. A series of four images from the Bar of Salvius ('Mr Safe Haven') features a man and woman brightly clad posed for a kiss; two drinkers arguing over wine; and a pair quarrelling over gambling, then being thrown out by the landlord.

An interesting take on the threat posed by such establishments comes from the emperor Trajan. Writing in a letter to Pliny, he noted that 'if people assemble for a common purpose, whatever reason, they soon turn into a political club'. Trajan's main concern, therefore, was not about the social ills of drinking, sex and gambling, but was instead political. He feared that elites gathering behind closed doors and being plied with food and wine might become susceptible to political persuasion and unite to become a threat.

DOWN AMONG THE DREGS

Some physical remains of this everyday life even survive today, allowing us to reconstruct shopping habits. One of the best is the desiccated remains of food that survive in storage vessels or containers found at preserved city sites like Pompeii and Herculaneum, where they are either built into the counters of bars or located nearby. Lentils were found at the bottom of a bronze container; other vessels held turnip seeds, cooked beans, onions, legumes, chickpeas, walnuts, rice and shellfish. A jar found in a *garum* shop in Pompeii contained the dried residue of that fish sauce that constituted one of the essential elements of the Roman diet. When researchers first opened the vessel, they were met with the faint odour of fish, a smell that transported them almost 2,000 years back in time and connected them to a world of shopping and the underbelly of human life.

The *garum* shop of Pompeii

This *garum* workshop was first discovered on Via di Castricio in Pompeii in 1958. It was connected to the distribution rather than the manufacture of the fish sauce so beloved in Roman cuisine.

Another rich seam of evidence is the cesspits and drains of ancient urban archaeological sites that expose, quite literally, the underside of shopping. Stratigraphic excavations of the sedimentary layers of debris and fecal matter using advanced techniques have recovered microscopic botanical materials. Analyses of excrement and latrine environments in Pompeii and Herculaneum have revealed a fruit-rich diet of figs, cherries, grapes and mulberries, and the evidence of soakaways (holes lined with rubble to allow water drainage) in Pompeii highlights the prevalence of shellfish in the diet.

·16·

WICKED STEPMOTHERS

———

Agrippina, the fourth wife of the emperor Claudius and stepmother
to his three children from previous marriages

Wicked stepmothers are all about
Roman inheritance...

A TRADITION OF EVIL

Wicked stepmothers have a notable place in the history of Western culture – think Cinderella and Snow White – and the trope has surprisingly deep roots. The idea of a stepmother working with some degree of malevolence – ranging from niggardly to homicidal – took a particularly potent and unique form in the Roman empire.

The historical evidence for a Roman stereotype of step-mothers being unusually malicious or hard-hearted is impressive for its variety and quantity. The oldest manifestation is in one of the earliest of any examples of Roman literature – Plautus's play *Pseudolus*, from c.200 BCE. In it, Ballio, a pimp, has a run-in with Calidorus, the son of a gentleman, whose lover, a prostitute, has been sold to a new master. Calidorus has no money to save her and his request for help is refused by Ballio, who goes on to ridicule him for his 'love and pinching want... You come empty-handed; words don't chink. But I wish you life and health.'

Rubbing his point in, the unpleasant Ballio then offers the observation that Calidorus's request is as hopeless as petitioning a stepmother:

> He's with these speeches really dead to me.
> When his procurer's pleas'd, a love lives.
> Be your complaint to me, a monied one
> For this same want of cash, which you lament
> So deeply, tell your story to your stepmother.

Plautus (c.254–184 BCE)

Titus Maccius Plautus was a Roman playwright famed during the Old Latin period for his comedies, which are among the earliest Latin literary works to have survived. The term 'Plautine drama' refers not only to his own works, but also to plays influenced by his style of writing. He wrote over 120 plays, only 20 of which survive, which were popular at the time they were produced (at the height of the Roman republic), and reflect contemporary events.

Similar examples survive in Roman literature throughout the empire. One of the latest comes from writings of the Christian priest and historian St Jerome (c.347–420 CE), whose collection of epistles or letters is one of the most important sources on life and belief in the late Roman empire. Writing half a millennium later than Plautus, St Jerome comments on stepmothers in a letter to Furia, a Roman widow:

You will not be allowed to love your first children, nor to look kindly on those to whom you have yourself given birth. You will have to give them their food secretly; yet even so your present husband will bear a grudge against your previous one and, unless you hate your sons, he will think that you still love their father. But your husband may have issue by a former wife. If so when he takes you to his home, though you should be the kindest person in the world, all the commonplaces of rhetoricians and declamations of comic poets and writers of mimes will be hurled at you as a cruel stepmother. If your stepson fall sick or have a headache you will be calumniated as a poisoner. If you refuse him food, you will be cruel, while if you give it, you will be held to have bewitched him. I ask you what benefit has a second marriage to confer great enough to compensate for these evils?

Jerome thus sees great danger for Furia in Rome if she changes her status to stepmother by remarrying a man with children. He advises her, in no uncertain terms, to remain a widow, and in so doing he makes clear the existence of an established popular tradition of mistrust.

A LEGAL STEREOTYPE

Another significant body of evidence comes from the *controversiae*, speeches in fictitious court cases designed to teach young Roman law students the art of rhetoric. Historians believe that, although these speeches are imaginary, they reflect many aspects of social situations that one would have encountered in everyday life. They are a particularly good source of prejudice and stereotyping: alongside wicked stepmothers, characters in the *controversiae* include pirates who kidnap someone's son or daughter; rivalry between rich and poor men; mothers protecting their children from tyrannical fathers; and fathers burdened with the difficulties of bringing up a dissolute or sober son. Young lawyers were taught to base their arguments around appealing to such stock characters in imaginary courts: the characters' stereotypical behaviour and beliefs were a rock on which to build the logic of their case. How do tyrants behave? They abuse their status and power. How do stepmothers behave? Well, they abuse their stepchildren, and favour their own children.

This is cleverly summed up in the *Declamatio Minor*, ascribed to the educator and rhetorician Quintilian. The case is set up like this: a childless woman, newly married to a man with children from a previous marriage, poisons herself to become infertile so that she cannot bear children with her new husband. The protagonist thus physically prevents herself from the temptation of favouring her own offspring over her new husband's children from his previous marriage. The husband finds out and disowns her, and thus they find themselves in court. Her jurist then lays out the case and makes it clear that his client's position is made difficult because there is pre-existing bias to overcome:

> Did she prepare poison, did she plot against your children, or what is the least of them, did she try to turn your mind against them? None of these. The charge is novel, never before heard of: a stepmother is said to love her stepsons too much.

The jurist thus makes it clear that the idea of a stepmother loving her stepsons so much is ridiculous, it is 'novel, never before heard of' – the implication being that stepmothers would always favour their own children.

INHERITANCE THEFT

In modern Western culture, the everyday cruelty of the wicked stepmother is emphasized, but in Roman sources the wickedness had a very specific and different focus: her avarice over the property of her new husband. The malevolence usually manifested itself in the stepmother seeking to secure for her own children, or sometimes for herself, the inheritance of her husband – and she did this either by causing a rift between him and his children, or, in the most extreme form, by killing his children, usually with poison.

Roman men were notably free from restrictions over where they might bequeath their inheritance. They could distribute it unevenly within the family; they could leave a substantial portion of it outside the immediate family; they could bequeath it to free women, who were allowed to own and inherit property and make wills of their own. This was made all the more significant by the high proportion of remarriages in the Roman empire, which can be explained by the low life expectancy: it was common for one's husband or wife to die young. Remarriage was also particularly significant among the upper classes for political reasons; marriage throughout the empire was a way of cementing alliances, building wealth and gaining power among the social elite. These new matches, however, were complicated by issues of inheritance, relating to the transfer of property and wealth. This in turn led to an increased awareness of – and sensitivity over – the legal problems posed by remarriage, a reflection of the real fear that it created.

A stepmother, therefore – especially one with children of her own from a previous marriage – had a great deal to fight for. If she played her cards right, she could claim the inheritance of her new husband for any of her children – regardless of the identity of their father – and even for herself if she was childless. There are suggestions that this type of manoeuvring occurred, though few real facts. The acclaimed Roman jurist Gaius (fl.130–180 CE), wrote of how fathers made 'spiteful judgements about their own flesh and blood after being corrupted by stepmotherly blandishments and promptings'. At the same time, however, it is noticeable that stepmothers bore the brunt of these anxieties when it could have been directed elsewhere – stepchildren and stepfathers were innocent as lambs in this tradition, when of course they could have been equally as culpable as the stepmothers.

LIVIA

One of the most interesting *real* examples of a stepmother who was framed as being evil was Livia (58 BCE–29 CE), wife of and adviser to the emperor Augustus. In almost all historical and literary depictions, her behaviour is described in a way that fits a stereotype of a wicked stepmother, an interpretation of her life that can be traced back to the historian Tacitus. In his *Annals*, his history of the empire from the reigns of Tiberius to Nero written around 117 CE, she is described as 'an oppressive mother to the nation', a view echoed by two other significant Roman historians – Suetonius and, a little later, Cassius Dio.

Livia certainly ensured that her bloodline, above anyone else's, would prosper. She only had one pregnancy with Augustus, but her son Tiberius, from her first marriage, entered into his step-father's inheritance and became emperor. She thus became the matriarch of the Julio-Claudian dynasty: the mother of Tiberius, grandmother of Claudius, great-grandmother of Caligula and great-great-grandmother of Nero. All of this happened because, at the start of the chain, her son's competitors – some with far better claims to Augustus's inheritance than Tiberius – all died, and when he gained power in 14 CE, others who threatened his position also died. There was certainly a heavy weight of circumstantial evidence that fitted the preconception of the wicked stepmother idea, but modern historians believe the case against her to be decidedly shaky.

Careful and considered historical research shows that her name was swirled in gossip, rumour and insinuation, but there are few hard accusations or facts. Of far more historical weight is the fact that she was the mother of an unpopular emperor, was loathed by those who opposed the Julio-Claudian dynasty and wanted her name destroyed, and had acquired more power than was deemed appropriate for a woman in a misogynistic society. Indeed, the stereotyping of women such as Livia as evil stepmothers tells us more about the society in which they lived than it does of the women themselves.

·17·
FEET

━━━━━

Roman footprint in an ancient tile from the kilns of the Tenth Legion in
Berg en Dal, near Nijmegen, Netherlands, c.70–103 CE

Feet are all about the Roman population…

ROMAN SHOES

We can tell much about the nature of the Roman population by what they wore on their feet. Archaeologists have uncovered thousands of examples of ancient footwear. One of the most interesting shoe hoards, for what it tells us about the population of a specific location, was excavated in 2016 by archaeologists working at the fort of Vindolanda in Northumberland, where they discovered a hoard of 421 shoes – all well-preserved in the site's damp anaerobic soil, and by this time almost 1,800 years old. The excavation of the site began in the 1930s, and since then researchers there have uncovered more than 6,000 shoes.

The fort was built as part of Hadrian's Wall during the fierce border wars fought between the ancient Britons and Roman forces from the second half of the first century CE. When the war ended in 212 CE, the occupants left the place that had once been their home, and as they did so they threw everything they could not carry into the fort's defensive ditch – which effectively became a rubbish dump. It was then covered over and sealed when the next settlement grew up in the fort's place, preserving it intact for almost two millennia.

What is remarkable about this particular collection of shoes is the sheer variety, which includes types that would have been worn by men and women as well as by children. In addition to the heavy-soled hobnailed sandal-boots or *caligae* worn by Roman soldiers are a range of indoor and outdoor shoes: baby boots, smaller shoes worn by children and teenagers, ladies' and men's boots, and clogs worn for bathing. Most shoes were made of leather, and among the hoard are some very well-made and stylish shoes, indicating the taste and affluence of some of Vindolanda's inhabitants.

The survival of such a large range of shoes, with over 40 per cent likely to have belonged to women and girls, suggests that the fort was not simply garrisoned by male soldiers accompanied by a number of prostitutes or female slaves, but that Vindolanda was a bustling and very mixed community with women (presumably wives) and children living alongside the soldiers. Indeed, the fact that there are so many women's shoes among the hoard offers evidence that women would have trodden the same ground as the Roman army.

Vindolanda

Occupied between roughly 85 and 370 CE, Vindolanda was first constructed as a frontier fort, and in the early 120s became a construction base for Hadrian's Wall. After the wall was completed Vindolanda formed part of the garrison for the wall, and played a major role throughout the wall's history.

A WALK FROZEN IN TIME

Much rarer finds are Roman footprints themselves, which survive in very small numbers but are tantalizing and powerful as moments from the ancient world, frozen in time. We know how people walked, since literary sources mention people taking a walk and visual sources depict them, but all too often this most basic of human activities leaves little material trace. One exception has also been found at Vindolanda. Among the remains uncovered at the site is a 2,000-year-old tile discovered in 2015 during a summer-school excavation. Impressed into the clay is what archaeologists believe to be the footprint of an adolescent, made at some point around 160–180 CE.

Another example survives in the Yorkshire Museum – the print of a hobnail-booted Roman soldier who trod on a setting floor tile in the Roman town of Eboracum, which evolved into what is now York. A human footprint and a hobnailed shoe-print also survive in a tile from Fishbourne Roman Palace near Chichester in Sussex, dating from the third century. Further examples of military footprints have been discovered in Israel, at the Hippos-Sussita archaeological site east of the Sea of Galilee. Here again it is the markings made by hobnails – the standard footwear for Roman legionaries was the tough leather *caliga* sandal-boot, with nails in the soles for grip – that have survived intact. Whether accidents or intentional pranks, such imprints in what would have been wet tiles are rare physical evidence of the practice of walking, and are as close as we can get to walking in the footsteps of the population of the Roman empire.

ANIMALS' FEET

It is not just human feet that have been frozen in time – a number of animal prints dating from ancient Rome survive in floor tiles, with the animals having padded over the wet clay. The Yorkshire Museum contains another example from Roman Eboracum, this time the paw prints of a dog impressed into brick. Measuring about seven centimetres in size, the animal's claws are quite visible today.

One of the largest collections of animal footprints uncovered by archaeologists is from the Roman site of Kefar 'Othnay (Legio) in Israel, near to the location of a Roman camp of the Sixth Legion Ferrata in the Jezreel Valley which dates from c.200 CE. The prints of five carnivores – cats, dogs and badgers – were found among the domestic structures of the settlement: four on tiles and one on a clay pot, discernible from the unique claw marks left behind. It is thought that the animals walked over the newly made tiles as they were laid down to dry. The cat's paw found on the surface of the pot is particularly charming – it might have been made by the animal leaning against or even pawing at the pot, or else by stretching up to paw the drying jar on a rack, perhaps in search of a snack. In combination with the zooarchaeological evidence of animal bones, historians have been able to reconstruct a picture of the movements of domestic and non-domestic animals that lived and roamed around this site and the immediate area.

VOTIVE FOOTPRINTS

Alongside footsteps captured in wet clay, a common feature of ancient statuary and stonework throughout the Roman empire is outlines of feet chiselled into stone, which are found in both religious and secular contexts. One particular form of footprint functioned as a votive offering, meant to be left to the gods. Such prints are known as *plantæ pedum* and are common across the Roman empire. They occur in various forms: sometimes a pair of matching feet, or rows of single feet, or even pairs of different feet (representing a mother and child or goddess and follower). Some are simple outlines, and others feature the more specific details of toes, toenails, and even footwear such as sandals. They could be carved in deep relief into stone or merely incised; and they appear in different patterns of orientation, either leading to or from the temple or statue.

One interesting example of feet imprinted in stone comes from a temple dedicated to the Egyptian goddess Isis (who was adopted by the Romans as a foreign goddess) in Baelo Claudia in southern Spain, and dates from the Flavian period (69–96 CE). In the first step of a stairway approaching the church are two plaques, each with a single carved relief of one stone foot, along with an inscription to the goddess. The feet are shown facing away from the temple, perhaps evidence of Isis greeting the worshippers, while the plaques are meant to be read by those approaching.

Votive offerings

Objects displayed or deposited in sacred sites for religious purposes, without the intention of recovery or use, as gifts to gain favour with deities. Votive offerings were a common feature of Roman religious beliefs and practices, and have been found within temples as well as in hoards.

·18·

INKWELLS

Ancient Roman ceramic inkwell (c.100 CE) found in Darion, Belgium

Inkwells are all about Roman power...

WRITING AND POWER

The written word in the ancient world was an important instrument of power and had a long-term impact on the organization and structure of society. While much could be done through oral communication and word of mouth, Roman elites and bureaucrats achieved power through written texts – including censuses, laws and even histories – and then exercised that authority in such crucial realms as business, land ownership, religion, government at home and abroad, and organizing the army and navy. Writing was also important in more personal relationships, between clients and patrons, within friendships and amorous relationships, and in the running of households. The ability to write gave a person the means to influence and change their world. An understanding of Roman literacy, therefore, is fundamental to our understanding of the Romans.

THE EVIDENCE OF LITERACY

As historians, we are able to measure literacy in various ways. Some fabulous examples of handwritten documents survive from the ancient world, but not in vast quantities. For later historical periods, signatures are used as a universal measure of literacy rates over time, but they are rare for the Roman period. Graffiti on ancient buildings and monuments does hint at plebeian literacy, but to be able to further explore the important question of who could read within Roman society we must examine the writing tools that have survived, as well as illustrations of them.

Writing was associated with a range of objects and materials, such as papyrus (used as a writing surface), seal boxes, styli, reed pens and ink. But such organic materials survive only in exceptional cases. What exists in much greater numbers across the Roman empire is the inkwell. Astonishingly, hundreds of examples have been discovered in a variety of contexts, including a particularly well-preserved ceramic inkwell dating from around 100 CE, discovered in Darion, Belgium. It is relatively simple in form – a small round pot with a narrow opening to prevent the ink from spilling.

Images of inkwells also appear on tombstones and other funerary monuments, as well as in Campanian wall paintings in the south of Italy, where the *theca calamaria* – a portable leather writing set comprising an inkwell, pens and styli – was commonly used by educated individuals as symbol of their learning.

Ownership of these writing technologies and the mastering aspects of their use – being able to make ink, cut a reed pen, sign one's name, form basic letters of the alphabet, write in complex Latin – gave people different levels of control over knowledge and the organizational systems that were the very basis of power throughout the Roman world.

Reed pen

A reed pen was a writing implement or stylus cut and shaped from a length of reed. The nib would be cut into a point and then split to take ink. Among the earliest surviving examples are from fourth-century BCE Egypt; reed pens were used throughout Roman society.

THE NATURE OF INKWELLS

Roman inkwells that survive vary enormously, and it is in this variety as well as in the details of where they are found that we can find tantalizing clues about who owned them – and therefore which groups within Roman society had control over writing systems.

They are generally made from metal. Among the most numerous in terms of type are more than 440 cast in bronze, which have formed the basis of an important recent study. Other examples are made of copper, and more rarely silver, as well as glass, ceramic and leather. Wooden inkwells also survive, but less frequently, and it is highly likely that horn was used too – as it was in medieval cultures – although examples are not extant.

They came in all sorts of different shapes and sizes. Some were cylindrical, while others hexagonal; some were tall and thin, and others short, squat and round. The openings varied greatly too: the more basic had a simple round top; some featured rotating apertures; and others had narrow entry points, just the right size to allow a writer to dip a nib in. Some were fashioned with handles and lids for portability, and these features came in a wide range of designs.

Those made of precious metals would have functioned as a luxury item, an expression of status; some were ornately decorated with a scroll or vine motif, and would perhaps have adorned a Roman desk – which was itself a status symbol. Leather inkwells formed part of portable writing sets. Occasionally a maker's name can be seen on the inkwell; one surviving bronze example contains a punched inscription which warns 'bad red ink'.

Dual inkwells allowed writers to use different-coloured inks for the demands of record-keeping, in which red and black had particular scribal functions. Red was normally the ink used for headings in official records.

In terms of size, it has been estimated that the average capacity for an inkwell was around 330 millilitres, which would represent a significant amount of ink. Even small inkwells of around 30 millilitres would have allowed the writer to produce a relatively lengthy amount of writing; larger inkwells may have been used by groups of professional scribes working together, which permits us to speculate about the bureaucratic organization of writers producing documents connected with government.

GEOGRAPHIES OF LITERACY

What is perhaps most remarkable about these inkwells is that their survival is an empire-wide phenomenon, which attests to the spread of the written word throughout the Roman world. At least ten recorded examples have been discovered in each of the sites of Cologne in modern-day Germany, Vindonissa in Switzerland, Magdalensberg in Austria, London in England, Intercisa in Hungary, Nijmegen in the Netherlands and the Italian city of Pompeii.

Vindonissa

A Roman legion camp established in 15 CE in the location of modern-day Windisch in Switzerland. The Thirteenth Legion was stationed there until 44 or 45 CE, and the camp was extended to incorporate almost thirty thermal baths.

As the capital, Rome sought to extend its reach and impose systems and order even at the outermost limits of the empire, and it did so not only through the might of the Roman army but also through the power of the pen. We thus find evidence of writing implements in the far north of England, with inkpots and a metal-nibbed pen found at the fort of Vindolanda, where archaeologists also uncovered very rare examples of fragments of tablets with ink marks, one of which was a letter sent along with some socks and sandals. The presence of such writing tools at the far reaches of Roman-controlled territory illustrates how writing was exported throughout the empire as a form of communication and control.

More information is uncovered if we look at *precisely* where these inkwells were found, which allows us to detail the kinds of groups that were literate. A significant number of inkwells have been found at military sites, including auxiliary forts – such as Loughor in Glamorgan, Wales, and Saalburg in Hesse, Germany – as well as legionary fortresses, like Longthorpe near Peterborough in Cambridgeshire, or Vindonissa in Switzerland. These finds are related to the importance of literacy and numeracy within the army – connected to recruitment, promotion, campaigning and provisioning.

Another site at which a significant number of inkwells survive is the Austrian hilltop settlement of Magdalensberg, which was occupied from the early first century BCE. Over time, it grew into a sizeable Roman town with large numbers of municipal and private buildings, and became a significant regional centre of trade and administration. Writing was clearly associated with this major urban centre. In addition to metal and ceramic inkwells, over 500 styli made out of bone and metal, as well as seal boxes, have been discovered there. This writing equipment was excavated in locations within the town associated with domestic households as well as official and business activities.

Clearly forts, towns and cities were populated by groups that produced an inordinate amount of paperwork. This is not, however, to suggest that writing was restricted to the metropolis, the mercantile and the military, for finds also occur in smaller settlements, villas and rural areas, where familiarity with the written word would have facilitated communication, bureaucracy and routine, as well as enabling more personal forms of writing within the household.

WOMEN WRITERS

The evidence of inkwells and other physical objects associated with writing has also enhanced our perception of women's writing skills, since a far greater number of such objects survive associated with women than was previously thought. Traditional estimates have viewed women as largely illiterate; they were powerful literary influences as muses, but thought on the whole not to have been skilled with pen and ink themselves. New evidence and interpretations, however, have begun to change our understanding of female literacy levels, and by implication have caused us to reassess the kinds of roles that women could undertake and the power that they could exercise.

One striking example is an image on a tombstone in Rome – it depicts a butcher's wife, seated in a high-backed chair, writing what are assumed to be the business accounts onto wax tablets. We also know that women were praised as 'educated mothers' and that they were trained to be teachers and scribes. Letters written by women have survived, with important examples found at Vindolanda in the UK and Tebtunis in Egypt. One such example is a Latin letter sent to Sulpicia Lepidina, wife of a commander stationed at Vindolanda, from her friend Claudia Severa, inviting her to visit to celebrate her forthcoming birthday.

Grave finds provide evidence that suggests the existence of literate Roman women. A recent survey of more than 125 graves that contain writing equipment, from locations across Europe and dating from the first to fourth centuries CE, reveals a significant number associated with women. Of the remains found in the forty-five graves where excavators have attempted to attach a gender, sixteen were thought to be female, and a number of those have since been osteologically proven to be female.

Of these, a grave in Vindonissa contains the body of a woman thought to be between eighteen and twenty-five years old, who was buried with a three-year-old child. Interred along with the bodies was a series of objects, including an inkwell and tweezers, glass and ceramic vessels, pig bones, and two coins dating from the mid-first century CE. On the basis of these artefacts, archaeologists have suggested that the occupant of the grave may have been a female doctor, who perhaps specialized in women's illnesses and childbirth. The Greek physician Soranus, who later practised in Rome, considered literacy as an important skill for midwives.

·19·
DEMONIC
POSSESSION

Beware the Dog mosaic at the entrance to the House of the
Tragic Poet in Pompeii, second century BCE

*Demonic possession is all about the rise
of Christianity...*

INSANITY AND DEMONS

The Roman understanding of mental illness changed over time. Early opinion was influenced by the general conception of health, which was based on the idea of the 'humoral' imbalance. It was believed that the body consisted of four different fluids: blood, yellow bile, black bile and phlegm, and their 'balance' – the proportion in which they existed inside a person's body – determined that person's health. In terms of mental health, a surplus of yellow bile would cause a violent mania, an excess of phlegm a quiet mania, and a surplus of black bile would produce melancholy. In fact, the word 'melancholy' itself has origins in the ancient world – the Greek word μέλᾰν or *melas* meaning 'black' and χολή or *khole* meaning 'bile'.

With the rise of Christianity in the empire, however, Christian writers began to explain mental disorders in terms of supernatural forces: that people's abnormal behaviour was caused by being possessed by demons – anonymous and unpredictable entities of uncertain power and identity, which were believed to exist everywhere and constantly affected human life.

An interesting anecdote that highlights the belief in demons and possession comes from the writing of Plutarch, a Greek biographer who became a Roman citizen. His story involves a man who escapes justice by appearing to be possessed:

> But just as they were ready to arrest him, an assembly
> of the citizens was held, and here Nicias, right in the
> midst of some advice that he was giving to the people,
> suddenly threw himself upon the ground, and after a little
> while, amid the silence and consternation which naturally

prevailed, lifted his head, turned it about, and spoke in a low trembling voice, little by little raising and sharpening its tones. And when he saw the whole audience struck dumb with horror, he tore off his mantle, rent his tunic, and leaping up half naked, ran towards the exit from the theatre, crying out that he was pursued... No man venturing to lay hands upon him or even to come in his way, out of superstitious fear, but all avoiding him, he ran out to the gate of the city, freely using all the cries and gestures that would become a man possessed...

His wife, who was also in on the scheme, took her children with her, 'prostrated in supplication before the temples of the Gods' and then left to find him. So appalled were the citizens at his behaviour that she was not followed, and so Nicias and his family escaped.

A WAR AGAINST EVIL

Learned reflections on demons were part of Christian theology from the earliest days of the religion. Christians of the time believed demons to be responsible for a great number of the world's ills, but they also believed that they were weak: if a person had become possessed by a demon, it could be expelled by the authority of Christ through the practice of exorcism. In a letter addressed to the 'Rulers of the Roman Empire' in which he defended his faith, the Christian author Tertullian wrote:

Let a person be brought before your tribunals, who is plainly under demoniacal possession. The wicked spirit, bidden to speak by a follower of Christ, will readily make the truthful confession that he is a demon, as elsewhere he has falsely asserted that he is a god.

Exorcism was tied up with the story of Jesus, who had performed the act with his disciples. It was vividly described – nine times for Jesus acting as an exorcist alone – in the Gospels and Acts of the Apostles. Early Christians were in no doubt that they were in the thick of a cosmic war, in which God and his angels were pitted against a variety of evil forces. In his letter to the Ephesians, believed to have been written around 80–100 CE, Paul the Apostle wrote:

> Our struggle is not against the enemies of blood and flesh,
> but against the rulers, against the authorities, against
> the cosmic powers of the present darkness, against the
> spiritual forces of evil in the heavenly places.

By the second century CE, exorcism was an established part of baptism, and historical accounts of exorcism of demons in the real world are seen to increase. The demons were often surprisingly domestic or familiar – this was not a time of fantastic demonic animals, but of demonic flies, mice and dogs.

DEMON DOGS

One extraordinary account survives in the *Life of St Theodore of Sykeon*, a hermit and ascetic (d.613 CE) whose biography was written by one of his disciples after 641 and is a key source for life under the rule of Heraclius, emperor of the eastern empire from 610 to 641. The *Life...* describes how when Theodore was travelling, he passed an inn. The innkeeper heard that he was close and sent for him, as 'he had been lying halfdead for a long time and his face was twisted right round to the back'. This clearly needed some explanation. The reason given was this:

> I was standing outside my inn, sir, when a black dog came
> up and stood in front of me and yawned, which made me

quite against my will yawn in the same way, and forthwith the dog disappeared from my sight! Directly afterwards I was seized with fever, I took to my bed and my face was turned round backwards.

Luckily for the man with the backwards head, Theodore knew exactly what to do:

the blessed man prayed over him and blew three times into his mouth, and after blessing some water he gave it to him saying, 'Drink some of this and rub yourself with it; for the thing you saw which cast a spell upon you was a demon; but in the name of Christ I hope we shall find you well when we return from our pilgrimage.'

Such descriptions of canine demons were common. Dogs appear as demons in pre-Christian Jewish, Greek and Roman folklore. This imagery arises from the fact that in the ancient world they were not the domestic pets that we know and love today, but rather lived wild, scavenging on what they could find. They were known to roam burial grounds outside the city walls, prisoners to their urges. In this way, they signified the lowest of the low of the animal world; the exact opposite of humans.

COLLECTIVE MADNESS

In 560, the Syrian ecclesiastical historian John of Ephesus (c.507–c.588 CE) described the fate of Amida, the Mesopotamian city in which he was born. Amida is now the Turkish city of Diyarbakir, located on the banks of the Tigris river on the border with Iraq. In antiquity, it was on the troubled border between Rome and Persia. At the time, John was in Constantinople, but he knew his city well and wrote his own version of the events that took it over.

People, he wrote, began to 'bark like dogs', as well as imitating the voices 'of all dumb animals'. Others made bizarre sounds 'as if with horns and trumpets', and cursed 'as if from devils in person'. Such uncontrolled and bizarre noises broke the calm of civilization. Deranged groups of citizens gathered together and stumbled around, and were seen ranging the burial grounds at night: notably canine behaviour. Some sang, some shouted, some – again in canine fashion – bit each other. Shame and conscience were absent, with the crowds exhibiting public displays of sexual cavorting and blasphemy. Some even foamed at the mouth.

All of these symptoms were accepted signs in the Christian world of demonic possession, and to John the presence of demons was clear. He despaired of how 'vicious demons might greatly control the youth to the extent of entrapping them in committing filthy debauchery among themselves inside the churches'.

In search of an explanation, modern-day historians have emphasized the repeated and horrific stresses that the inhabitants of Amida had been under for half a century. In 502, the city was captured from Rome by the Persians, who massacred 80,000 of its inhabitants; two years of war followed as the Romans fought to recapture the city. Under the Roman siege, the citizens suffered appallingly from starvation and abuse at the hands of their new Persian overlords. By 505 Amida was back in Roman hands, but there were constant raids and skirmishes to contend with. The citizens, moreover, were of a particular branch of Christian faith known as Monophysitism, and they became subject to horrific religious persecution under the new bishop of Amida, Abraham bar Kaili, who imposed the beliefs of the new holy Roman emperor, Justinian (c.482–565 CE).

Then, in 543, the city was infected with plague, resulting in some 30,000 deaths in just three months. An eight-year famine followed. In 560, just before the outbreak of the madness, false rumours of a new Persian invasion led to mass migration, civic chaos and fear.

Monophysitism

A branch of Christian belief which held that Christ's divinity and humanity were united, as opposed to Chalcedonian beliefs, which held that they were separate. Following the Council of Chalcedon 451 CE, which asserted Catholic orthodox doctrine, the Monophysites, who were mostly found in Egypt and Mesopotamia, were branded heretics and persecuted to varying degrees, depending on the emperor and the archbishop responsible for their region.

The citizens of Amida reached breaking point. Bereft of all hope and faith in religious or secular protection, they behaved as if they had been abandoned by God – to the extent that they appeared to have been possessed. The remedy, according to John, was a mixture of carefully chosen foods as medicines, taken with a healthy dose of Christian religion. The sick were gathered in churches and calmed through penitence, religious ritual and pilgrimage, and it was effective. John wrote that 'one by one and little by little they started to come to their senses. They grieved, wept, groaned and kept busy in prayer and in painful supplication at all time.'

·20·

THE NUMBER SEVEN

The seven hills of ancient Rome, eighteenth century

The number seven is the key to the
Roman universe…

The Romans saw the number seven everywhere: in their present, in their past, on earth and in the heavens. The Roman author and philosopher Aulus Gellius (c.125–after 180 CE) noted that 'in many natural phenomena a certain potency and possibility of the number seven has been observed', and the philosopher Philo (c.25 BCE–c.50 CE), who lived in Roman Egypt, asked 'for what part of the universe is not enamoured of seven, overcome by desire and longing for the number seven?' Seeing significance in its ever-presence, the Romans repeatedly wrote about it, celebrated it, and even enshrined it in the geography of Rome itself.

PREGNANCY AND GROWTH

An author who explored the contemporary interest in the number seven more than any other was the Roman scholar Marcus Varro, who had been inspired by ancient lists that he had come across: the philosophers of ancient Greece known as the Seven Sages; the Greek play *Seven Against Thebes* (467 BCE); the Seven Wonders of the World. Varro consequently committed a fifteen-volume book, *Hebdomades vel De Imaginibus*, entirely to the occasions that the number seven could be identified in nature, and also to categorizing things, and people, in groups of seven,

The work is mentioned by both Pliny the Elder in his *Naturalis Historia* and by the author Aulus Gellius in his work *Attic Nights*, a fascinating compendium of contemporary thought and history. Gellius tells us that, in his first volume, Varro tackled 'the many varied excellencies and powers of the number seven', but unfortunately reveals no more about what those excellencies and powers might be. We do learn, though, that Varro saw seven as being central to many things of great significance to the Romans – including the cosmos, the zodiac, disease and death – and he took particular note of the number seven in the context of conception and pregnancy. Occasionally, Gellius quotes directly from Varro, and he does so in this instance to explain the significance of the number seven in relation to the development of a foetus in the womb:

> For when the life-giving seed has been introduced into the female womb, in the first seven days it is compacted and coagulated and rendered fit to take shape. Then afterwards in the fourth hebdomad [meaning a group of seven days] the rudimentary male organ, the head, and the spine which is in the back, are formed. But in the seventh hebdomad, as a rule, that is, by the forty-ninth day, the entire embryo is formed in the womb.

He further notes:

> that before the seventh month neither male nor female child can be born in health and naturally, and that those which are in the womb the most regular time are born two hundred and seventy-three days after conception, that is, not until the beginning of the fortieth hebdomad.

Varro's observations about the number seven and human growth continued after birth. The teeth, he said, appear in the first seven months and then fall out within seven years, and the 'back teeth' are then added within twice seven years. He also claimed that 'the extreme limit of growth of the human body' was seven feet.

IN HEAVEN

Human creation was not the only mystery that could be unlocked by the number seven. For Roman astrologers, the number seven was literally written into the heavens. A complete lunar cycle lasted twenty-eight days and each of the four distinct lunar phases lasted for seven days, defining a 'week'. Moreover, five planets had been identified by this period – which, in addition to the sun and the moon, made seven. Together, they gave their names to the days of the week:

Sunday (*dies Solis*)	Sun
Monday (*dies Lunae*)	Moon
Tuesday (*dies Martis*)	Mars
Wednesday (*dies Mercurii*)	Mercury
Thursday (*dies Iovis*)	Jupiter
Friday (*dies Veneris*)	Venus
Saturday (*dies Saturni*)	Saturn

This seven-day week was formally adopted by the emperor Constantine in 321 CE, but it had informally been in use by the Romans since the first century BCE, and beyond that can be traced back to the Babylonian civilization in Mesopotamia.

The seven-day lunar phases and the number of the planets (which he called 'wandering stars') did not escape the attention of Varro, and he noted several other important points about the number seven in the heavens. He observed that the constellations of the Greater Bear and Lesser Bear were marked out by seven stars, and so too was the constellation known to the Romans as the *Virgiliae* – otherwise known as the 'Pleiades' or the 'Seven Sisters' – which is the cluster of stars most visible to the naked eye. He also saw seven in the passage of the year. Gellius again recalled Varro's ideas:

> the summer solstice occurs in the seventh sign from the winter solstice, and the winter solstice in the seventh after

the summer, and one equinox in the seventh sign after the other. Then too those winter days during which the kingfishers nest on the water he says are seven in number.

SEVEN HILLS

One of the most interesting manifestations of this obsession with the number seven appears in the identification of Rome's 'seven' hills. Rome is known worldwide today as the 'City of Seven Hills', and there is literary evidence that it was associated with seven hills from as early as the second half of the first century BCE. The Greek historian Dionysius of Halicarnassus (c.60–after 7 BCE) noted that the sixth king of Rome, Servius Tullius (ruled c.575–535 BCE), was the first to build a wall around the city, and that in so doing he 'surrounded the seven hills with one wall'.

But how many hills does Rome actually have? The answer, if you look at its geography, is not seven: it is possibly as many as thirteen, depending on precisely who you ask. Certainly there is the Palatine Hill which, according to Roman mythology, was where the twins Romulus and Remus – who were central to the founding of the city – were found in a cave. The hill became the location of several emperors' palaces, including those of Augustus, Tiberius and Domitian, as well as the great stadium the Circus Maximus, home to Rome's famed chariot races. There is also the Capitoline Hill, the ceremonial centre of the city and home to several important temples – most importantly the enormous Temple of Jupiter, which became a symbol of the city itself. And then there is the Aventine Hill to the south, another that was linked to the myth of Romulus and Remus, and which also became associated with the city's poorest inhabitants – the plebs – just as the Palatine became linked with emperors.

Romulus and Remus

In Roman mythology, they are the twin brothers whose story is connected to the events that led to the founding of the city of Rome. Seeing them as a threat to his rule, King Amulius ordered them to be killed, and they were abandoned on the banks of the Tiber to die. However, they were saved by the god Tiberinus, brought up by a she-wolf, and later found by a shepherd. It was on the site they were abandoned that the two of them built what was to become the city of Rome.

If you look at Rome's geography, at least ten more individual hills can be identified. But so important were the positive associations with the number seven in the Roman world that what mattered most to the Romans was not how many hills there actually were, but that there were seven. Modern historians believe that, by associating their city with the number seven, the Romans were placing their city at the centre of the universe.

So powerful has the reputation of Rome's seven hills been over the centuries, that numerous other cities around the world – including some of history's greatest cultural hotspots – have made a similar claim, drawing their strength from the example of imperial Rome. They include Jerusalem, Mecca, Athens, Edinburgh, Liverpool, Bristol, Bath, Kiev, Prague, Moscow, Madrid, Lisbon, Budapest, Istanbul, Rio de Janeiro and Kampala; and in the US, San Francisco, Cincinnati, Seattle and Richmond, Virginia.

It is fitting that, just like in Rome, the reality of there being seven hills in each of these cities is very much open to debate; what matters more than the reality is the number and the desire for these modern cities – as culturally polarized as Jerusalem, Moscow and San Francisco – to associate themselves with Rome as a model of urban civilization.

JOIN IN!

We believe passionately that everyone – not just professional historians – can effectively exercise their historical imagination. If you have a great idea for a *Histories of the Unexpected* subject, fill in one of these forms, photograph it and send it to us

on Twitter **@UnexpectedPod**

or by email to **info@historiesoftheunexpected.com** and we might dedicate a podcast episode to you and your historical imagination!

The history of _____ is all about...

_____

The history of _____ is all about...

_____

The history of _____ is all about...

_____

The history of _____ is all about...

_____

The history of _____ is all about...

_____

SELECTED FURTHER READING

GENERAL

Beard, Mary, *SPQR: A History of Ancient Rome* (London: Profile Books, 2015).

Birley, Robin, *Vindolanda: Extraordinary Records of Daily Life on the Northern Frontier* (Greenhead, Northumberland: Roman Army Museum Publications, 2005).

Boardman, John, Jasper Griffin and Oswyn Murray, eds, *The Oxford History of the Roman World* (Oxford: Oxford University Press, 1991).

Coulston, J. C., and Hazel Dodge, eds, *Ancient Rome: The Archaeology of the Eternal City* (Oxford: Oxford University School of Archaeology, 2000).

Dupont, Florence, *Daily Life in Ancient Rome* (Oxford: Blackwell Publishers, 1993).

Flower, Harriet I., ed., *The Cambridge Companion to the Roman Republic* (Cambridge: Cambridge University Press, 2004).

Goldberg, Sander, ed., *The Oxford Classical Dictionary* (digital edition) (New York: Oxford University Press, 2016).

Kelly, Christopher, *The Roman Empire: A Very Short Introduction* (Oxford: Oxford University Press, 2006).

Le Glay, Marcel, et al., *A History of Rome* (3rd edition) (Oxford: Wiley, 2004).

Morley, Neville, *Ancient History: Key Themes and Approaches* (London: Routledge, 1999).

Peachin, Michael, ed., *The Oxford Handbook of Social Relations in the Roman World* (Oxford: Oxford University Press, 2011).

Potter, David S., ed., *A Companion to the Roman Empire* (Oxford: Blackwell Publishers, 2006).

Ramage, Nancy H., and Andrew Ramage, *The Cambridge Illustrated History of Roman Art* (Cambridge: Cambridge University Press, 1991).

Rosenstein, Nathan S., and Robert Morstein-Marx, eds, *A Companion to the Roman Republic* (Oxford: Blackwell Publishers, 2006).

Syme, Ronald, *The Roman Revolution* (Oxford: Oxford University Press, 2002).

Treggiari, S., *Roman Social History* (London: Routledge, 2002).

Wacher, John, ed., *The Roman World*, 2 vols (London: Routledge, 1987).

Woolf, Greg, ed., *The Cambridge Illustrated History of the Roman World* (Cambridge: Cambridge University Press, 2003).

WEBSITES

BBC History, 'Romans', http://www.bbc.co.uk/history/ancient/romans/ [accessed 22.03.19].

Pompeii Archaeological Park, http://pompeiisites.org/ [accessed 22.03.19].

Vindolanda Archaeological Site, http://www.vindolanda.com/ [accessed 22.03.19].

1. WALLS

Aldrete, Gregory S., *Daily Life in the Roman City: Rome, Pompeii, and Ostia* (Westport, CT: Greenwood Press, 2004).

Baird, Jennifer, and Claire Taylor, eds, *Ancient Graffiti in Context* (London: Routledge, 2010).

Beard, Mary, *Pompeii: The Life of a Roman Town* (London: Profile Books, 2008).

Benefiel, Rebecca R., 'Dialogues of Ancient Graffiti in the House of Maius Castricius in Pompeii', *American Journal of Archaeology*, 114/1 (2010), pp. 59–101.

Bergmann, B., 'Exploring the Grove: Pastoral Space on Roman Walls' in *The Pastoral Landscape*, ed. J. D. Hunt (Washington, DC: University Press of New England, 1992), pp. 21–46.

Dey, Hendrik W., *The Aurelian Wall and the Refashioning of Imperial Rome, AD 271–855* (Cambridge: Cambridge University Press, 2011).

Franklin, James L., 'Games and a Lupanar: Prosopography of a Neighborhood in Ancient Pompeii', *The Classical Journal*, 81/4 (1984), pp. 319–28.

Historic England, 'Written Rock of Gelt: Roman Quarry Inscriptions', https://historicengland.org.uk/listing/the-list/list-entry/1014582 [accessed 01.03.19].

Joshel, Sandra R., and Lauren Hackworth Petersen, *The Material Life of Roman Slaves* (Cambridge: Cambridge University Press, 2014).

Levin-Richardson, Sarah, '*Facilis hic futuit*: Graffiti and Masculinity in Pompeii's "Purpose-Built" Brothel', *Helios*, 38/1 (2011), pp. 59–78.

McGinn, Thomas A. J., *The Economy of Prostitution in the Roman World: A Study of Social History & the Brothel* (Ann Arbor, MI: University of Michigan Press, 2004).

Milnor, Kristina, *Graffiti and the Literary Landscape in Roman Pompeii* (Oxford: Oxford University Press, 2014).

Ohlson, Kristin, 'Reading the Writing on Pompeii's Walls', *Smithsonian Magazine* (26 July 2010), https://www.smithsonianmag.com/history/reading-the-writing-on-pompeiis-walls-1969367/ [accessed 01.03.19].

Ovid, *Metamorphoses*, trans E. J. Kenny (Oxford: Oxford University Press, 2008).

Tybout, R. A., 'Roman Wall-painting and Social Significance', *Journal of Roman Archaeology*, 14 (2001), pp. 33–56.

Varone, Antonio, *Eroticism in Pompeii* (Los Angeles, CA: J. Paul Getty Museum, 2001).

2. TATTOOS

Carr, Gillian, 'Woad, Tattooing and Identity in Later Iron Age and Early Roman Britain', *Oxford Journal of Archaeology*, 24/3 (2005), pp. 273–92.

Gustafson, W. M., '*Inscripta in fronte*: Penal Tattooing in Late Antiquity', *Classical Antiquity*, 16 (1997), pp. 79–105.

Hambly, W. D., *The History of Tattooing and its Significance* (London: H. F. & G. Witherby, 1925).

Jones, C. P., '*Stigma*: Tattooing and Branding in Graeco-Roman Antiquity', *Journal of Roman Studies*, 77 (1987), pp. 139–55.

Kamen, Deborah, 'A Corpus of Inscriptions: Representing Slave Marks in Antiquity', *Memoirs of the American Academy in Rome*, 55 (2010), pp. 95–110.

Leighton, Albert C., 'Secret Communication among the Greeks and Romans', *Technology and Culture*, 10/2 (1969), pp. 139–54.

Treherne, P., 'The Warrior's Beauty: The Masculine Body and Self-Identity in Bronze-Age Europe', *Journal of European Archaeology*, 3/1 (1995), 105–44.

3. POSTURE

Corbeill, Anthony, *Nature Embodied: Gesture in Ancient Rome* (Princeton, NJ: Princeton University Press, 2004).

——, 'Dining Deviants in Roman Political Invective', in Judith P. Hallett and Marilyn B. Skinner, eds, *Roman Sexualities* (Princeton, NJ: Princeton University Press, 1997), pp. 99–128.

Graf, F., 'The Gestures of Roman Actors and Orators' in J. Bremmer and H. Roodenburg, eds, *A Cultural History of Gesture from Antiquity to the Present Day* (New York: Polity Press, 1991), pp. 36–58.

Roller, Matthew B., *Dining Posture in Ancient Rome: Bodies, Values, and Status* (Princeton, NJ: Princeton University Press, 2017).

———, 'Horizontal Women: Posture and Sex in the Roman Convivium', *The American Journal of Philology*, 124/3 (2003), pp. 377–422.

4. TAMING

Blackman, Deane R., and A. Trevor Hodge, eds, *Frontinus' Legacy: Essays on Frontinus' de aquis urbis Romae* (Ann Arbor, MI: University of Michigan Press, 2001).

Brown, S., 'Death as Decoration: Scenes from the Arena on Roman Domestic Mosaics' in Amy Richlin, ed., *Pornography and Representation in Greece and Rome* (Oxford: Oxford University Press, 1992).

Jennison, George, *Animals for Show and Pleasure in Ancient Rome* (Philadelphia, PA: University of Pennsylvania Press, 2005).

Purcell, Nicholas, 'Rome and the Management of Water: Environment, Culture and Power' in G. Shipley and J. Salmon, eds, *Human Landscapes in Classical Antiquity: Environment and Culture* (London: Routledge, 1996), pp. 180–212.

Shelton, Jo-Ann, 'Beastly Spectacles in the Ancient Mediterranean World' in L. Kalof, ed., *A Cultural History of Animals in Antiquity* (Oxford: Berg Publishers, 2007), pp. 97–126.

Wilson, A., 'Water, Power and Culture in the Roman and Byzantine Worlds: An Introduction', *Water History*, 4/1 (2012), pp. 1–9.

———, 'Deliveries *Extra Urbem*: Aqueducts and the Countryside', *Journal of Roman Archaeology*, 12/1 (1999), pp. 314–31.

5. RECYCLING

Barker, S., 'Marble Salvaging during the Roman Period', in Anna Gutiérrez Garcia-M., Pilar Lapuente Mercadal and Isabel Rodà de Llanza, eds, *Interdisciplinary Studies on Ancient Stone:*

Proceedings of the IX ASMOSIA Conference (Tarragona: Institut
Català d'Arqueologia Clàssica, 2012), pp. 22–30.

——, 'Roman Builders – Pillagers or Salvagers?: The Economics
of Deconstruction and Reuse' in S. Camporeale et al., eds,
*Arqueología de la construcción II. Los procesos constructivos en el
mundo romano: Italia y provincias occidentales* (Madrid: Archivo
Español de Arqueología, 2011), pp. 127–42.

——, and C. Ward, 'Roman Stone-carvers and Re-carving:
Ingenuity in Recycling', in Patrizio Pensabene and Eleanora
Gasparini, eds, *Interdisciplinary Studies on Ancient Stone:
ASMOSIA X: Proceedings of the Tenth International Conference*
(Rome: L'Erma di Bretschneider, 2015), pp. 765–78.

Ng, Diana Y., and Molly Swetnam-Burland, eds, *Reuse and
Renovation in Roman Material Culture: Functions, Aesthetics,
Interpretations* (Cambridge: Cambridge University Press, 2018).

Paynter, S., and C. M. Jackson, 'Re-used Roman Rubbish: A
Thousand Years of Recycling Glass', *Post-Classical Archaeologies*,
6 (2016), pp. 31–52.

Penn Museum, 'The Puteoli Marble Block', https://www.penn.
museum/collections/highlights/mediterranean/puteoli-
marble-block.php [accessed 28.02.19].

Swift , E., 'Object Biography, Re-use and Recycling in the Late to
Post-Roman Transition Period and Beyond: Rings Made from
Romano-British Bracelets', *Britannia*, 43 (2012), pp. 167–215.

6. WALKING

Adkin, N., 'The Teaching of the Fathers Concerning Footwear and
Gait', *Latomus*, 42 (1983), pp. 885–6.

Brown, R. D., 'The Litter: A Satirical Symbol in Juvenal and Others'
in Carl Deroux, ed., *Studies in Latin Literature and Roman History*,
Vol. III (Brussels: Peeters Publishers, 1983), pp. 266–82.

Fowler, D., 'Laocoon's Point of View: Walking the Roman Way'
in S. J. Heyworth, P. G. Fowler and S. J. Harrison, eds, *Classical*

Constructions: Papers in Memory of Don Fowler, Classicist and Epicurean (Oxford: Oxford University Press, 2007), pp. 1–17.

Sullivan, Timothy M., *Walking in Roman Culture* (Cambridge: Cambridge University Press, 2011).

Vindolanda Trust, 'Ancient Footprint Discovery Leaves Lasting Impression at Vindolanda', http://www.vindolanda.com/_blog/press-releases/post/ancient-footprint-discovery-leaves-lasting-impression-at-vindolanda/ [accessed 11.02.19].

7. POISON

Jones-Lewis, Molly Ayn, 'Poison: Nature's Argument for the Roman Empire in Pliny the Elder's *Naturalis Historia*', *The Classical World*, 106/1 (2012), pp. 51–74.

Juvenal, *The Satires*, trans. Niall Rudd (Oxford: Oxford University Press, 1992).

Kaufman, David B., 'Poisons and Poisoning among the Romans', *Classical Philology*, 27/2 (April 1932), pp. 156–67.

Nepovimova, Eugenie, and Kamil Kuca, 'The History of Poisoning: From Ancient Times until Modern ERA', *Archives of Toxicology*, 93/1 (January 2019), pp. 11–24.

Nriagu, Jerome O., 'Saturnine Gout Among Roman Aristocrats – Did Lead Poisoning Contribute to the Fall of the Roman Empire?', *The New England Journal of Medicine*, 308 (March 1983), pp. 660–3.

Olson, Kelly, 'Cosmetics in Roman Antiquity: Substance, Remedy, Poison', *The Classical World*, 102/3 (Spring 2009), pp. 291–310.

Paule, Maxwell Teitel, *Canidia, Rome's First Witch* (London: Bloomsbury Academic, 2017).

Van Hooff, Anton J. L., 'Ancient Euthanasia: "Good Death" and the Doctor in the Graeco-Roman World', *Social Science & Medicine*, 58/5 (2004), pp. 975–85.

8. THE KISS

Clarke, John R., *Looking at Lovemaking: Constructions of Sexuality in Roman Art, 100 B.C.–A.D. 250* (Berkeley, CA: University of California Press, 1998).

Courthope, W. J., *Epigrams of Martial* (Cambridge: Chadwyck-Healey, 1992).

Henig, M., *A Handbook of Roman Art: A Survey of the Visual Arts of the Roman World* (Oxford: Phaidon, 1983).

Laes, Christian, and Ville Vuolanto, *Children and Everyday Life in the Roman and Late Antique World* (London: Routledge, 2010).

Monnickendam, Y., 'The Kiss and the Earnest: Early Roman Influences on Syriac Matrimonial Law', *Le Muséon*, 125/3–4 (2012), pp. 307–34.

Penn, Michael Philip, *Kissing Christians: Ritual and Community in the Late Ancient Church* (Philadelphia, PA: University of Pennsylvania Press, 2005).

Scioli, E., *Dream, Fantasy, and Visual Art in Roman Elegy* (Madison, WI: University of Wisconsin Press, 2015).

Steinlauf, N. T., 'The Kiss in Roman Law', *Classical Journal*, 41/1 (1945), pp. 24–37.

9. COLLECTING ART

d'Ambra, E., *Art and Identity in the Roman World* (London: Weidenfeld & Nicolson, 1998).

Bounia, Alexandra, *The Nature of Collecting in the Classical World: Collections and Collectors, c.100 BCE–100 CE* (Leicester: University of Leicester, 1998).

Campbell, Gordon Lindsay, ed., *The Oxford Handbook of Animals in Classical Thought and Life* (Oxford: Oxford University Press, 2014).

Farkas, A., et al., eds, *Monsters and Demons in the Ancient and*

Medieval Worlds: Papers Presented in Honor of Edith Porada (Mainz: Philipp von Zabern, 1987).

Mheallaigh, Karen ní, *Reading Fiction with Lucian: Fakes, Freaks and Hyperreality* (Cambridge: Cambridge University Press, 2014).

Miles, Margaret M., *Art as Plunder: The Ancient Origins of Debate about Cultural Property* (Cambridge: Cambridge University Press, 2008).

Rutledge, S. H., *Ancient Rome as a Museum: Power, Identity, and the Culture of Collecting* (Oxford: Oxford University Press, 2012).

Strong, D. E., *Roman Museums: Selected Papers on Roman Art and Architecture* (London: Pindar Press, 1994).

10. SOLAR POWER

Hannah, Robert, and Giulio Magli, 'The Role of the Sun in the Pantheon's Design and Meaning', *Numen*, 58/4 (2011), pp. 486–513.

Hughes, J. D., *Environmental Problems of the Greeks and Romans: Ecology in the Ancient Mediterranean* (Baltimore, MD: Johns Hopkins University Press, 2014).

——, 'Ancient Deforestation Revisited', *Journal of the History of Biology*, 44/1 (2011), pp. 43–57.

Jordan, B., and J. Perlin, 'Solar Energy Use and Litigation in Ancient Times', *Solar Law Reporter*, 1/3 (1979), pp. 583–94.

MacDonald, William L., *The Pantheon: Design, Meaning, and Progeny* (Cambridge, MA: Harvard University Press, 2002).

Miliaresis, I., 'Heating and Fuel Consumption in the Terme del Foro at Ostia' (PhD thesis, University of Virginia, 2013).

Plommer, Hugh, *Vitruvius and Later Roman Building Manuals* (Cambridge: Cambridge University Press, 1973).

Ring, J. W., 'Windows, Baths, and Solar Energy in the Roman Empire', *American Journal of Archaeology*, 100/4 (1996), pp. 717–24.

University of Washington, 'Baths and Bathing as an Ancient Roman', https://depts.washington.edu/hrome/Authors/kjw2/

BathsBathinginAncientRome/pub_zbarticle_view_printable.
html [accessed 23.03.19].

11. FISH

Davaras, Costis, 'Rock-Cut Fish Tanks in Eastern Crete', *The Annual of the British School at Athens*, 69 (1974), pp. 87–93.

Higginbotham, J. A., *Piscinae: Artificial Fishponds in Roman Italy* (Chapel Hill: University of North Carolina Press, 1997).

Holleran, Claire, 'A Handbook to Shopping in Ancient Rome', *BBC History Magazine*, 18 December 2016, https://www.historyextra.com/period/roman/a-handbook-to-shopping-in-ancient-rome/ [accessed 04.03.19].

Horden, P., and N. Purcell, *The Corrupting Sea: A Study of Mediterranean History* (Oxford: Blackwell Publishers, 2000).

King, A. R., 'An Examination of the Economic Role of Table Fish in Ancient Rome' (MA dissertation, University of Kansas, 2013).

Marzano, Annalisa, *Harvesting the Sea: The Exploitation of Marine Resources in the Roman Mediterranean* (Oxford: Oxford University Press, 2013).

Purcell, N., 'Rome and the Management of Water: Environment, Culture and Power' in J. Salmon and G. Shipley, eds., *Human Landscapes in Classical Antiquity: Environment and Culture* (London: Routledge, 1996), pp. 180–212.

———, 'Eating Fish: The Paradoxes of Seafood' in J. Wilkins et al., eds, *Food in Antiquity* (Exeter: University of Exeter Press, 1995), pp. 132–49.

Reese, David S., 'Fish: Evidence from Specimens, Mosaics, Wall Paintings, and Roman Authors' in W. M. Jashemski and G. Meyer, eds, *The Natural History of Pompeii* (Cambridge: Cambridge University Press, 2002), pp. 274–91.

Toynbee, J. M. C., *Animals in Roman Life and Art* (London: Thames & Hudson, 1973).

Wilkins, J., 'Social Status and Fish in Greece and Rome' in Gerald

Mars and Valerie Mars, eds, *Food, Culture and History* (London: London Food Seminar, 1993), pp. 191–203.

——, and S. Hill, *Food in the Ancient World* (Oxford: Blackwell Publishers, 2006).

12. BENCHES

Epstein, David F., 'Caesar's Personal Enemies on the Ides of March', *Latomus*, 46/3 (1987), pp. 566–70.

Evans, Richard J., *Questioning Reputations: Essays on Nine Roman Republican Politicians* (Pretoria: University of South Africa Press, 2003).

Gorski, Gilbert J., and James E. Packer, *The Roman Forum: A Reconstruction and Architectural Guide* (Cambridge: Cambridge University Press, 2014).

Grant, Michael, *The Roman Forum* (London: Weidenfeld & Nicolson, 1970).

Hartnett, Jeremy Scott, 'Streets, Street Architecture, and Social Presentation in Roman Italy' (PhD thesis, University of Michigan, 2003).

More, T. J., 'Seats and Social Status in the Plautine Theatre', *Classical Journal*, 90 (1995), pp. 113–23.

Platner, Samuel Ball (as completed and revised by Thomas Ashby), *A Topographical Dictionary of Ancient Rome* (Oxford: Oxford University Press, 1929).

Rawson, E., '*Discrimina Ordinum*: The *Lex Julia Theatralis*', *Papers of the British School at Rome*, 55 (1987), pp. 83–114.

Rose, P., 'Spectators and Spectator Comfort in Roman Entertainment Buildings: A Study in Functional Design', *Papers of the British School at Rome*, 73 (2005), pp. 99–130.

Taylor, L. R., *Roman Voting Assemblies: From the Hannibalic War to the Dictatorship of Caesar* (Ann Arbor, MA: University of Michigan Press, 1966).

Zanker, Paul, *Pompeii: Public and Private Life* (Cambridge, MA: Harvard University Press, 1998).

13. WEAVING

Clark, Gillian, 'Roman Women', *Greece & Rome*, 28/2 (1981), pp. 193–212.

Edmondson, Jonathan C., and Alison Keith, eds, *Roman Dress and the Fabrics of Roman Culture* (Toronto: University of Toronto Press, 2008).

Gleba, M., and U. Mannering, eds, *Textiles and Textile Production in Europe from Prehistory to AD 400* (Oxford: Oxbow Books, 2012).

Gleba, M., and J. Pásztókai-Szeöke, eds, *Making Textiles in Pre-Roman and Roman Times: People, Places, Identities* (Oxford: Oxbow Books, 2013).

Harlow, Mary, 'Dressmaking the Roman Way', *Lucius' Romans Blog*, University of Kent, https://blogs.kent.ac.uk/lucius-romans/2016/12/15/dressmaking-the-roman-way/ [accessed 04.03.19].

———, 'Dressing to Please Themselves: Clothing Choices for Roman Women' in M. E. Harlow, ed., *Dress and Identity* (Oxford: Archaeopress Publishing, 2012), pp. 39–46.

———, and M. L. Nosch, eds, *Greek and Roman Textiles and Dress* (Oxford: Oxbow Press, 2014).

Heilbrun, Carolyn G., 'What was Penelope Unweaving?' in Heilbrun, *Hamlet's Mother and Other Women: Feminist Essays on Literature* (London: The Women's Press, 1991), pp. 103–11.

Hooper, Luther, 'The Technique of Greek and Roman Weaving', *The Burlington Magazine for Connoisseurs*, 18/95 (1911), pp. 276–9; 281–4.

Lowenstam, Steven, 'The Shroud of Laertes and Penelope's Guile', *Classical Journal*, 95/4 (2000), pp. 333–48.

Matthews, Kenneth D., 'The Imperial Wardrobe of Ancient Rome', *Expedition Magazine*, 12/3 (1970), Penn Museum, 1970, https://www.penn.museum/sites/expedition/the-imperial-wardrobe-of-ancient-rome/ [accessed 04.03.19].

Mueller, Melissa, 'Helen's Hands: Weaving for *Kleos* in the *Odyssey*', *Helios*, 37/1 (2010), pp. 1–21.

Olson, Kelly, *Dress and the Roman Woman: Self-Presentation and Society* (London: Routledge, 2008), pp. 16–20.

Ovid, *Metamorphoses*, trans. E. J. Kenny (Oxford: Oxford University Press, 2008).

Propertius, *Sextus Propertius: The Love Elegies*, trans. A. S. Kline (Liber Publications, 2001).

Scheid, John, and Jesper Svenbro, *The Craft of Zeus: Myths of Weaving and Fabric* (Cambridge, MA: Harvard University Press, 1996).

Sebesta, Judith Lynn, and Larissa Bonfante, eds, *The World of Roman Costume: Wisconsin Studies in Classics* (Madison, WI: University of Wisconsin Press, 1994).

14. FATTENING

Beerden, Kim, 'Roman Dolia and the Fattening of Dormice', *Classical World*, 105 (2012), pp. 227–35.

———, 'A Conspicuous Meal: Fattening Dormice, Snails, and Thrushes in the Roman World', *Petit Propos Culinaires*, 90 (2010), pp. 79–98.

Bradley, Mark, 'Obesity, Corpulence and Emaciation in Roman Art', *Papers of the British School at Rome*, 79 (2011) pp. 1–41.

Corbier, M., 'The Broad Bean and the Moray: Social Hierarchies and Food in Rome' in A. Sonnenfeld, ed., *Food: A Culinary History from Antiquity to the Present* (New York: Columbia University Press, 1999), pp. 128–40.

Daremberg, Charles, and Edmond Saglio, *Dictionnaire des antiquités grecques et romaines* (Paris: Librairie Hachette, 1877–1919).

Gowers, E., *The Loaded Table: Representations of Food in Roman Literature* (Oxford: Clarendon Press, 1993).

Varro, M. Terentius, *De Re Rustica*, trans. W. D. Hooper and H. B. Ash (Cambridge, MA: Harvard University Press, 1934).

Zanker, Paul, 'The Irritating Statues and Contradictory Portraits of Julius Caesar' in Miriam Griffin, ed., *A Companion to Julius Caesar* (Chichester: Wiley-Blackwell, 2009), pp. 288–314.

15. SHOPPING

Beard, Mary, 'Banter About Dildoes', *London Review of Books* (3 January 2013).

———, *Pompeii: The Life of a Roman Town* (London: Profile Books, 2008).

Corbier, M., 'The Broad Bean and the Moray: Social Hierarchies and Food in Rome' in *Food: A Culinary History from Antiquity to the Present*, pp. 128–40.

Ellis, Steven J. R., *The Roman Retail Revolution: The Socio-Economic World of the Taberna* (Oxford: Oxford University Press, 2018).

———, 'The Distribution of Bars at Pompeii: Archaeological, Spatial and Viewshed Analyses', *Journal of Roman Archaeology*, 17 (2004), pp. 371–84.

Holleran, Claire, 'A Handbook to Shopping in Ancient Rome', *BBC History Magazine*, 18 December 2016, https://www.historyextra.com/period/roman/a-handbook-to-shopping-in-ancient-rome/ [accessed 04.03.19].

———, 'Women and Retail in Roman Italy' in Emily Hemelrijk and Greg Woolf, eds, *Women and the Roman City in the Latin West* (Leiden: Brill, 2013), pp. 313–30.

———, *Shopping in Ancient Rome: The Retail Trade in the Late Republic and the Principate* (Oxford: Oxford University Press, 2012).

Theophrastus, *The Characters of Theophrastus*, ed. and trans. by J. M. Edmonds (London: Heinemann, 1929).

16. WICKED STEPMOTHERS

Dinter, M., et al., eds, *Reading Roman Declamation: The Declamations Ascribed to Quintilian* (Berlin: De Gruyter, 2016).

Dixon, S., *The Roman Mother* (London: Croom Helm, 1988).

Gray-Fow, M. J. G., 'The Wicked Stepmother in Roman Literature and History: An Evaluation', *Latomus*, 47/4 (1988), pp. 741–57.

Noy, D., 'Wicked Stepmothers in Roman Society and Imagination', *Journal of Family History*, 16/4 (1991), pp. 345–61.

Watson, P. A., *Ancient Stepmothers: Myth, Misogyny, and Reality* (Leiden: Brill, 1995).

17. FEET

Bar-Oz, Guy, and Yotam Tepper, 'Out on the Tiles: Animal Footprints from the Roman Site of Kefar 'Othnay (Legio), Israel', *Near Eastern Archaeology*, 73/4 (2010), pp. 244–7.

McComish, J. M., *A Guide to Ceramic Building Materials* (York: York Archaeological Trust, 2015), https://www.yorkarchaeology.co.uk/wp-content/uploads/2015/05/A-guide-to-ceramic-building-material-reduced.pdf [accessed 20.03.19].

Revell, Louise, 'Footsteps in Stone: Variability Within a Global Culture', in Susan E. Alcock, Mariana Egri and James F. D. Frakes, eds, *Beyond Boundaries: Connecting Visual Cultures in the Provinces of Ancient Rome* (Los Angeles, CA: Getty Publications, 2016), pp. 206–21.

van Driel-Murray, Carol, 'Vindolanda and the Dating of Roman Footwear', *Britannia*, 32 (2001), pp. 185–97.

18. INKWELLS

Eckardt, Hella, *Writing and Power in the Roman World: Literacies and Material Culture* (Cambridge: Cambridge University Press, 2019).

———, 'Writing Power: The Material Culture of Literacy as Representation and Practice' in Astrid Van Oyen and Martin Pitts, eds, *Materialising Roman Histories* (Oxford: Oxbow Books, 2017), pp. 23–30.

Eiseman, C. J., 'Classical Inkpots', *American Journal of Archaeology*, 79 (1975), pp. 374–5.

Howley, Joseph A., *Aulus Gellius and Roman Reading Culture: Text, Presence and Imperial Knowledge in the* Noctes Atticae (Cambridge: Cambridge University Press, 2018).

Khairy, N. I., 'Ink-wells of the Roman Period from Jordan', *Levant*, 12 (1980), pp. 155–62.

Starr, R. J., 'Reading Aloud: Lectores and Roman Reading', *Classical Journal*, 86 (1991), pp. 337–43.

Ullman, Berthold L., 'Illiteracy in the Roman Empire', *Classical Journal*, 29/2 (1933), pp. 127–8.

19. DEMONIC POSSESSION

Ahonen, M., 'Ancient Philosophers on Mental Illness', *History of Psychiatry*, 30/1 (2019), pp. 3–18.

Harvey, S. A., *Asceticism and Society in Crisis: John of Ephesus and the Lives of the Eastern Saints* (Berkeley, CA: University of California Press, 1990).

Metzger, Nadine, 'Kynanthropy: Canine Madness in Byzantine Late Antiquity', *History of Psychiatry*, 26/3 (2015), pp. 318–31.

Toner, J., *Roman Disasters* (Cambridge: Polity Press, 2013).

van Lommel, K., 'The Recognition of Roman Soldiers' Mental Impairment', *Acta Classica*, 56 (2013), pp. 155–84.

20. SEVEN

Clayton, P. A, and M. Price, *The Seven Wonders of the Ancient World* (London: Routledge, 2013).

Parker, H., 'The Seven Liberal Arts', *The English Historical Review*, 5/19 (1890), pp. 417–61.

Shanzer, D., *A Philosophical and Literary Commentary on Martianus Capella's* De Nuptiis Philologiae et Mercurii, Book 1 (Berkeley, CA: University of California Press, 1986).

Stahl, W. H., et al., eds, *Martianus Capella and the Seven Liberal Arts*, 2 vols (New York: Columbia University Press, 1971–7).

Vout, C., *The Hills of Rome: Signature of an Eternal City* (Cambridge: Cambridge University Press, 2012).

ILLUSTRATION CREDITS

p. 1 Fresco in the Villa dei Misteri, Pompeii (*Wikimedia Commons*); p. 11 Hadrian's Wall (*Dave Head/Shutterstock*); p. 13 Pyramus and Thisbe fresco from the House of Loreius Tiburtinus, Pompeii (*Wikimedia Commons*); p. 19 Remains of a Scythian warrior (*dpa picture alliance archive/Alamy Stock Photo*); p. 27 Fresco from Pompeii showing a banquet or family ceremony (*Wikimedia Commons*); p. 33 The Magerius Mosaic (*DeAgostini/Getty Images*); p. 41 The Puteoli marble block (*Penn Museum*); p. 49 Fresco of covered litter, Pompeii (*AGB Photo Library/Alamy Stock Photo*); p. 59 Wall painting of a woman from the Villa Farnesina, Pompeii (*Science History Images/Alamy Stock Photo*); p. 67 Sculpture of Cupid embracing Psyche (*Adam Eastland/Alamy Stock Photo*); p. 75 Marble statue of a wounded Amazon (*Peter Horree/Alamy Stock Photo*); p. 83 Inside the Pantheon, Rome (*Viroj Phetchkhum/Shutterstock*); p. 89 Seventeenth-century plan of the Pantheon (*Public domain*); p. 91 Roman mosaic of fish and ducks (*PRISMA ARCHIVO/Alamy Stock Photo*); p. 99 The *schola* tomb of the priestess Mamia in Pompeii (*Erin Babnik/Alamy Stock Photo*); p. 107 Mosaic depicting Hercules and Omphale (*PRISMA ARCHIVO/Alamy Stock Photo*); p. 115 Emperor Vitellius depicted in a bronze plaque (*Azoor Photo/Alamy Stock Photo*); p. 120 Denarius coin depicting Julius Caesar (*Photo 12/Alamy Stock Photo*); p. 123 Relief from the port city of Ostia (*DEA/G. DAGLI ORTI/De Agostini via Getty Images*);

p. 131 Bust of Agrippina (*Adam Eastland/Alamy Stock Photo*); p. 139 Roman footprint in an ancient tile (*Wikimedia Commons*); p. 145 Ancient Roman ceramic inkwell (*age fotostock/Alamy Stock Photo*); p. 153 Beware the Dog mosaic, Pompeii (*khd/Shutterstock*); p. 161 Eighteenth-century plan of the seven hills of Rome (*Granger Historical Picture Archive/Alamy Stock Photo*)

While every effort has been made to contact copyright-holders of illustrations, the authors and publisher would be grateful for information about any illustrations where they have been unable to trace them, and would be glad to make amendments in further editions.

INDEX

Actium, Battle of (31 BCE), 45, 62

Aetius, 25

Agathocles, King of Syracuse, 80

Agrippa, Marcus Vipsanius, 45–6

Agrippina the Elder, 23

Agrippina the Younger, 51, 61, 65, 70–71

Alexander the Great, 44

ambulatio, 56–7

Amida, Mesopotamia, 157–9

Ammianus Marcellinus (historian), 118–19

amphitheatres, 101–102

ancient Britons, 24, 140

animals, 34–7, 142–3
　demon dogs, 156–7
　dormice, 116–19
　fattening, 116–18
　footprints, 142–3
　taming, 35–6

Annals (Tacitus), 137

Apelles, 44

Apicius (recipe collection), 118

Appius Claudius Pulcher, 56

Apuleius, 96

aqueducts, 38–40
　Aqua Appia, 38
　Aqua Augusta, 39
　Pont du Gard, Provence, 38
　Valens, Istanbul, 38

Aquila, Pontius, 106

Archimedes, 77

architecture, 84–90
　amphitheatres, 101–102
　bathhouses, 86–8
　heating, 84–6
　repurposing, 42–7

Ars Poetica (Horace), 127

art, 76–81

astrology, 163–4

Astyanax, 54

Athenaeus, 96

Attic Nights (Gellius), 162–3

Augustus, Roman emperor, 22, 32, 37, 39, 44, 45, 87, 102–3, 109–10, 136–7, 165

Aurelian, Roman emperor, 12

Aventine Hill, Rome, 165

Babylon, 13, 164

Baelo Claudia, Spain, 143

bar Kaili, Abraham, bishop of Amida, 158

bars, 126–8

Bar of Salvius, Pompeii, 127–8

bathhouses, 86–8

Bay of Naples, 18, 39

benches, 100–106

Boniface IV, Pope, 46

Britain, 3, 6, 12, 24

Britannicus, 32, 61

Brutus, Marcus Junius, 36–7

Caecilius Statius, 28–9

Caesar, Julius, Roman emperor, 24, 29, 31, 36–7, 54, 62, 104–6, 119

Caesarion, Pharaoh of Egypt, 54

Caesonia (wife of Caligula), 65

caldarium, 87

calendar, 163–4

Caligula, Roman emperor, 23, 65

Canidia, 60, 126

Capitoline Hill, Rome, 120, 165

Capitoline Museums, Rome, 30

Caracalla, Roman emperor, 8

Carthage, 4, 77

Catullus, 55, 69

Charlemagne, King of the Franks, 3

children, 54, 140–41

and posture, 32

stepchildren, 134–6

Chresimus, Titius, 40

Christianity, 9, 46–7, 72–3, 154–9

Monophysitism, 158–9

Chrysostom, John, Bishop of Constantinople, 73

Cicero, Marcus Tullius, 6, 28, 37, 54, 55–6, 79–81, 95

Cicero, Quintus Tullius, 50–51

Circus Maximus, Rome

citizens, 8

Claudius, Roman emperor, 44, 50–51, 61, 65, 71

Cleopatra, Pharaoh of Egypt, 54, 61–2

Clodia Pulchra (Metelli), 55–6, 69

Colloquia of the Hermeneumata Pseudodositheana, 92

Cologne, Germany, 149

Colosseum, Rome, 101–103

Commentary on Genesis (Ephrem), 71

Constantine, Roman emperor, 9, 23, 46, 164

Constantinople, 2–3, 38

controversiae, 134

convivium, 28, 32

Corinth, Greece, 78–9

cuisine, *see* food

Curia, 104–5

damnatio ad bestias, 35

damnatio memoriae, 42–3

Darion, Belgium, 147

De Architectura (Vitruvius), 87
De Bello Gallico (Caesar), 24
*De Diversis Fabricis
    Architectonicae* (Faventinus),
    85–6
De Poetis (Suetonius), 28–9
De Vita Caesarum (Suetonius),
    29
Declamatio Minor (Quintilian),
    134–5
demonic possession, 154–9
Digest of Justinian, 78, 88
dining practices, 28–32
Dio, Cassius, 121, 137
dolia, 117–18
Domitian, Roman emperor,
    43–5, 47, 64, 102, 165
dormice, 116–19

Eboracum (York), 142
Egypt, 97–8
Elegies (Propertius), 109, 113
Ephesus, Turkey, 47
Ephrem the Syrian, 71–2
Epigrams (Martial), 68
Epistles (Horace), 127
Epodes (Horace), 60, 127
erotic imagery, 17
exorcism, 156

Faventinus, Marcus Cetius,
    85–6
fish, 92–7, 128–9
    fish ponds, 93–5

Fishbourne Roman Palace,
    Sussex, 142
Flavian dynasty, 143
food, 116–19, 128–9
    dining practices, 28–32
footprints, 141–2
footwear, 125, 140–42
France, 38
freeborn, 7–8, 22, 25
friendship, 56
Frontinus, Sextus Julius, 39
funerals, 51

Gaius (jurist), 136
Gaius Sempronius Gracchus
    (politician), 52, 53
Galen, 25, 119, 125
garum, 97, 128–9
Gellius, Aulus, 162–4
Gemellus, Lucius Bellenus, 93
Gemonian Stairs, Rome, 120–21
Germanicus (general), 23
Germanicus (nephew of
    Tiberius), 60
gladiators, 23
gods, *see* religion
government, 3, 104–5
graffiti, 15–18, 146
graves, 151–2
    see also tombs
Greece, 6, 76, 78–9, 92

Hadrian, Roman emperor,
    45–6, 88

Hadrian's Wall, 12, 17, 140–41
Hannibal, 4
Hebdomades vel De Imaginibus (Varro), 162
Hector, 54
heliocaminus, 87–8
Heraclius, Roman emperor, 156
Herculaneum, 87, 128–9
Hermitage Museum, St Petersburg, 24
Herodas, 124–5
Herodian, 24
Heroides (Ovid), 113
Hippos-Sussita, Israel, 142
Historia Augusta, 36
Homer, 112
Horace, 6, 60, 126–7
Hortensius, 95
Hostilia, 63–4
houses, *see* architecture
humors, 154
hypocausts, 84

Iliad (Homer), 112
In Verrem (Cicero), 79
inkwells, 147–51
Intercisa, Hungary, 149
Israel, 142–3
Istanbul, *see* Constantinople
ius osculi, 70–71

John VII, Pope, 47
John of Ephesus, 157–9
Judaism, 9, 157

Julio-Claudian dynasty, 44, 61, 137
Justinian, Roman emperor, 158
Juvenal, 6, 64–5, 127

Kefar 'Othnay (Legio), Israel, 142–3
kissing, 68–73

Latin, 6, 133, 147
Lepidina, Sulpicia, 151
Lesbia, 69
Lex Aelia Sentia, 22
Lex Julia Theatralis, 102
Liber Spectaculorum (Martial), 36
Life of Augustus (Suetonius), 109
Life of St Theodore of Sykeon, 156–7
light, 88–90
literacy, 146–52
litters, 52–3
Lives of the Caesars (Suetonius), 23
Livia Drusilla, 109–10, 136–7
Livy, 63
Locusta, 60–61
London, England, 3, 149
Longthorpe, Cambridgeshire, 150
Loughor, Wales, 150
Lucretius, 96
Lucullus, Lucius Licinius, 94–5

Magdalensberg, Austria,
    149–50
Magerius Mosaic, 34–5
Maius Castricius, House of,
    Pompeii, 18
Marcellus, Marcus Claudius,
    76–7
Mark Antony, 31, 55, 62
marriage, 71, 136
Martial, 6, 25, 36, 52, 68–70, 93,
    95, 124
Martina, 60
Mediterranean Sea, 2
men, gait of, 53–5
mental illness, 154, 157–8
Mesopotamia, 157–9, 164
Metamorphoses (Ovid), 12–15,
    110
Midsummer Night's Dream, A
    (Shakespeare), 13
Milvian Bridge, Battle of the
    (312 AD), 9
Monophysitism, 158–9
Mummius, Lucius, 78–9
mythology, 2, 9, 54, 110–11,
    112–13, 165–6

National Archaeological
    Museum of Naples, 117
Naturalis Historia (Pliny the
    Elder), 97, 162
Nero, Roman emperor, 50–51,
    61
Nerva, Roman emperor, 39

Nijmegen, Netherlands, 149
Nobilior, Marcus Fulvius, 77

obesity, 119–21
Octavian, *see* Augustus, Roman
    emperor
Odes (Horace), 127
Odysseus, 112
Odyssey (Homer), 112
Oppian, 96
Orpheus, 30
Ottoman empire, 3
Ovid, 6, 12–15, 96, 110–11, 113, 126

paganism, 46–7
Palatine Hill, Rome, 165
Pallas, 50
Pantheon, Rome, 45–6, 88–90
patricians, 8
Pax Romana, 44–5
pedarii, 105
pedlars, 125–6
Penelope (wife of Odysseus),
    112–13
Penn Museum, Philadelphia,
    43
Petronius, 20–21, 126
Philippi, Battle of, (42 BCE), 127
Philo, 162
Philomela, 110–11
Phocas, Byzantine emperor, 46
physiognomy, 54–5
plantae pedum, 143
Plautus, 28, 132–3

plebeians, 8, 105
Pliny the Elder, 25, 62, 44–5, 94–7, 162
Pliny the Younger, 29, 51, 56–7, 85, 86, 128
Plutarch, 76, 108, 119, 154–5
poetry, 29
poison, 60–65
Polemon, 55
Polybius, 77
Pompeii, Italy, 87, 93, 100–101, 126–9, 149
grafitti, 15–18
Pompey, 36, 37, 106
Pomponius, 24
Pont du Gard, Provence, 38
posture, 28–32
Pozzuoli, Italy, 43
Praetorian Guard, 44
pregnancy, 163
Propertius, 70, 103, 108, 109, 113
prostitution, 17
Pseudolus (Plautus), 132
Punic Wars, 4
2nd Punic War (218–201 BCE), 77
3rd Punic War (149–146 BCE), 4
punishment, 22–3
Pyramus and Thisbe, 13–15

Quintilian, 119, 134–5

reed pens, 147
religion, 8–9, 46–7, 143–4

Res Rustica (Varro), 31, 116–17
Roman empire, 2–9
Roman republic, 2, 5
Rome (city), 2, 4, 51, 124
founding of, 166
seven hills, 165–7
Romulus and Remus, 2, 90, 104, 165, 166

Saalburg, Germany, 150
Santa Maria Antiqua, Rome, 47
Satires (Horace), 60, 127
Satires (Juvenal), 64–5
Satyricon (Petronius), 20–21
Scythians, 23–4
Senate, 104–5
Seneca the Younger, 12, 30, 54, 94, 110
Serapeum of Alexandria, 46
seven (number), 162–7
Seven Against Thebes (play), 162
Seven Sages, 162
Seven Wonders of the World, 162
Severa, Claudia, 151
sex
and graffiti, 17–18
and women, 30–31
erotic imagery, 17
prostitution, 17
Shakespeare, William, 13
shoes, *see* footwear
shops, 124–9

Sicily, 77, 79–80
slaves, 7–8, 20–22, 24–5, 30, 54, 78, 102
social status, 29–31, 50–54, 65, 93, 101–2, 118
society, 7–8
solar power, 85–8
soldiers, 5, 20, 22, 24, 140–42, 150
Solinus, Gaius Julius, 24
Soranus, 152
St Jerome, 133–4
St Paul, 156
St Theodore of Sykeon, 156–7
statues, 78, 80
  repurposing, 42–4
stepmothers, 132–7
Suetonius, 23, 28–9, 32, 70–71, 94, 102, 106, 109, 121, 137
Sulla, 36
Syracuse, Siege of (213–212 BCE), 76–7
Syro-Roman Lawbook, 71

Tacitus, 5, 51, 137
Tarpeian Rock, Rome, 105
tattoos, 20–25
  removal, 24–5
Tebtunis, Egypt, 151
Terence (Publius Terentius Afer), 28–9
Tertullian, 71–3, 155
theca calamaria, 147
Thracians, 23

Tiberius, Roman emperor, 94, 120, 137, 165
Tiberius Sempronius Gracchus, 53
timber, 84
'Time of the Kings', 2
Titus, Roman emperor, 32, 36
toga virilis, 32
tombs, 100–101
  tomb of Mamia, Pompeii, 100
  see also graves
Torre Astura, Italy, 93
Trajan, Roman emperor, 2, 39, 44–5, 51, 128
tribunes, 105–6
Tristia (Ovid), 113
Triumvirate
  First, 104–5
  Second, 45, 55

Ulpian, 88

Valens Aqueduct, Istanbul, 38
Valerius Maximus, 22, 30–31
Varro, Marcus Terentius, 30, 31, 94, 108, 116–18, 162–4
Vegetius, 22
venationes, 35
Verres, Gaius, 79–81
Vestal Virgins, 102–3
Vindolanda fort, Northumberland, 5–6, 140–42, 150, 151

Vindonissa, Switzerland,
149–50, 152
Virgil, 6
Vitellius, Roman emperor,
120–21
Vitruvius, 86, 87
votive offerings, 143–4
feet, 143–4

walking, 50–57, 141
walls, 12–18
war, 76
water, 38–40
weaving, 108–13

woad, 24
women, 7, 102
and inheritance, 135–6
and kissing, 70–71
and poison, 60–65
and posture, 30–32
and sex, 30–31
stepmothers, 132–7
and walking, 54, 55–6
and weaving, 108
writers, 151–2
writing, see literacy

Yorkshire Museum, York, 142